Praise for Kris Radish

"Through the women in her popular novels, author Kris Radish reveals what has value and meaning in her life—friendships and a passion for living."
—*Albuquerque Journal*

"Radish unrolls a rollicking yet reflective read that adds to her robust repertoire of beloved fiction. What's a reader to do but relish the ride."
—*BookPage on Searching for Paradise in Parker, PA*

"Kris Radish creates characters that seek and then celebrate the discovery of … women's innate power."
—*The Denver Post*

"In Radish's book, everything takes on a meaning that is larger than life … Radish's books are also a little like the cliff-hangers of the 1920s, with one page pulling you to the next…."
—*Lansing City Pulse*

"Radish's … characters know how to have a good time on their way to matriarchal nirvana."
—*Kirkus Reviews*

"A funny and provocative attempt to nudge numb, stagnant, and confused souls into a new direction."
—*Capital Times*

Gravel on the Side of the Road

True Stories from a
Broad Who Has Been There

Kris Radish

SparkPress, a BookSparks imprint
A division of SparkPoint Studio, LLC

DEDICATION

This one has been a long time coming and is for all those brave hearts and souls who opened their lives to me and trusted me to tell their stories. I have never forgotten you and remain grateful for your trust.

The Radish Broad's Stories

Introduction

Ordinary is often very extraordinary but experiences in this realm are usually overlooked. Although my life has been far from ordinary, many of my experiences are just that—wonderfully ordinary.

A touch of a baby's hand, the line of light fading into the arms of darkness at twilight, the first time you realize you love someone, the moment your child reaches out in a gesture of simple fondness that breaks your heart with the weight of emotion.

That is life. Your life. My life. All our lives.

My life also continues to be extraordinary. I am a writer, an author, and a journalist who prods the folds of the world for every piece of life that I can swallow. I have been to war in Bosnia and held the hands of dying babies. I have walked the often-tense lines between being totally objective and making certain someone knows I am a human being. People have tried to kill me and rape me and push me off cliffs. I have fallen from the sky and landed on the shoulders of hundreds of goddesses.

All these stories, all the times that I have danced with the FBI and held hands with the world's underbelly, have added to the vitality of my own spirit. These experiences, no matter how small, have helped me move from one phase of my life to the next and have helped me maintain my stride. That is what I call extraordinary.

Just walk quietly and we will slip past her before she even knows we are here." Once, I swear to God, a cougar jumped the entire width of the road and I memorized its track and my wild-man friend, who knew every animal in the world, told me yes, that was a cougar.

Tonight there is a car waiting at the gate. It is a black Thunderbird totally out of place in this world of beat-up trucks and foreign cars that are normally used for target practice and I am torn between backing up and seeing who the hell is at the gate.

I am not a small or a large woman but somewhere in between. Tall. Fast legs. A little thin but definitely not the kind of broad who will make a man cry for help. Any goofball could push me over if he tried hard enough but I am always thinking that I would be able to maim him first so the cops would recognize him. "Look at that scar," the policemen would say. "This poor son of a bitch must have been up at the gate."

Today, like always, I have a stick the size of a baseball bat alongside me in the car in case a tribe of crazed hula dancers tries to overtake me but how can I hide this weapon under my blue down jacket if I need to beat the hell out of someone without them knowing it?

Thinking nothing but, "golly gee," like a trusting fool, I pull close to this car, just to its left side, and get out. It is winter but there is no snow on the ground and the wind here, higher than in the valley, cuts into my face and slaps me awake.

My shoes crunch on the frozen gravel as I edge around my car door, stepping like I am one of those damned deer who think I never see them. I'm smart enough at least to keep the door open in case I have to pull a Lois Lane and run like hell. I approach the Thunderbird cautiously.

As a journalist people pay me to observe things, and I memorize the license plate, and then I look for strange marks on the car so I can scratch something about what I notice into the dirt when I lie bleeding to death on the frozen gravel. There are two heads in the front seat. One head is very low and I realize it is a child, a young boy, maybe about thirteen years old. What the hell?

The other passenger is a man who rolls down the window after I tap on it to get his attention. He is gone to his happy place. His movements are fluid and practiced like he is telling himself, "Okay, move your arm and then your lips." His pupils are dilated but I can't smell marijuana so he must be in a much deeper and more severe happy place than the rest of the potheads I have come to know and love.

The boy looks nervous. He also looks frightened. His shoulders are hunched over, his hands are tucked between his thighs, and he is trying not to look anyone in the eye. Father and son? An abducted neighbor boy? A runaway? What the hell?

My inner voices are beginning to rage. Their sounds are like gurgling fountains that are about to erupt. "Get the holy hell out of there!" they are trying to tell me, but I choose to play out my hand, even though I do not have a full deck myself.

"Hello," I say calmly, far enough away from the window so that he can't grab me.

"Hello," he says, and his voice is surprisingly clear. I see his fingers tap-dancing on the steering wheel. He's thinking very hard and very fast.

"Can I help you?"

"I don't know."

This is going good so far. I have not seen any machetes, machine guns, or sawed-off shotguns, but the interior of the car is kind of dark.

"Well, who are you?"

This is the million-dollar question and when I ask it this guy turns his head and sticks it out of the window so he looks like a little duck bobbing for air after a frosty dip.

"I'm Jesus."

Well, I am not dressed for this encounter. My nails look like shit and I am dying for a glass of beer but here it is, my first interview with Jesus, and wouldn't you know it, I'm not prepared.

"Jesus?"

"Yes, I am Jesus."

This is not how I imagined it. I want a choir and beautiful angels rubbing my shoulders. I want to be suddenly razor thin, have my acne scars evaporate, and I want to have long blonde hair that curls around my shoulders. It would also be nice to have my legs shaved and all my bills paid and to maybe have done something remarkable with my pathetic life.

"Who are you?"

Here is where I blow it. Here is where I cannot help but be the smart-ass woman that I am. Here is where I always get in trouble. You can count on this as sure as you can count on Republicans to be conservative and women to always have to struggle for every single thing they need and want and deserve.

"Well, if you really are Jesus you would know who I am."

This agitates Jesus to no end. He is now pissed but I think fast.

"I can get a key to the gate. Is that what you want?"

"Yes," he says, clearly relieved. "I need to get in quickly."

"Is something going on?"

"People are up there—they are waiting for me. Lots of people."

This is why my drug of choice is a cold beer. It is bad enough just being myself. Can you imagine this conversation if I were stoned out of my mind?

"Listen, I'm going to go get the key and I'll be right back. Wait here. Just, well, pray or something."

Holy shitski! I lunge for my car and begin backing up to the neighbor's ranch, which is about half a mile away. I'm really good at this because often in the winter I gun the living hell out of the car and drive backward through the gate so I can coast past the snowdrifts when I have to leave in the morning. Well, okay, sometimes I run off the sides of the road and I have to stick my one good jacket or the car blanket or the car mats under the wheels to get out, but I always seem to get where I need to be.

My neighbor, Ron, is home and he has the longest pistol I have ever seen in my life. When he tucks it into his pants I am surprised it does not come out at the top of his black leather cowboy boot.

"Jesus," I tell him gasping for breath. "He's at the gate."

This strikes none of us as funny because we live in a place where people like to do bad things. They drive up the canyon and try to rape each other. They throw kittens out of their car windows and push garbage into my streams. They tromp through places that are not meant for human feet and they try to steal things that they could never use in a million years. Jesus at the gate is not a funny thing. Not yet. Not until we are safe.

Ron heads up to meet Jesus alone and Joy, his wife, passes me a cold beer and asks if I can help them pick night crawlers later that week. This is something I do for extra money. I put a little headlight on top of my hat and crawl around in the horse fields and pick night crawlers. Believe it or not, it is not the worst way I have made money. I will think about this particular job the rest of my life, especially when I am broke, and when people do not buy my stories, and when I feel sorry for myself. I will often say, "Hey, stupid, you could be picking night crawlers."

But I will also remember how calm it was in the middle of the night when I was in the fields. I'll remember how the night crawlers poked their heads out and then I grabbed them and how I would count each one—ten cents, twenty cents, I just made a dollar. I will remember how I wore my jeans through at the knees and how I stood in the shower when I got home until I could feel blood rushing again through my frigid veins. I will remember how I threw my head back and laughed so hard thinking about what I looked like crawling around in the fields, just like an animal myself, and I will always remember how I loved the mountains where the worms moved unafraid and how I cried the day I left.

Back to Jesus.

Joy and I are pacing, but she has confidence in this man of hers, because she doesn't know yet that he is screwing a woman much younger than she is, who lives down in the valley and is already pregnant with his baby. Joy, with the polio that makes her legs work like an unbalanced seesaw, who has kind eyes, and who falls for stupid-ass men and who has never had more than two pairs of shoes her entire life. Joy doesn't really need Jesus right now either.

Ron comes back very quickly and tells us that Jesus has decided to leave.

"Who was he?"

"Some damn fool."

"Did he tell you anything?"

"Nope. I just pulled back my jacket and showed him the gun and he left."

"I can't believe he waited for me to come back."

"That's Jesus for you."

Later that night, I am waiting for nothing but the morning. It is dark outside and I have the porch light on for company. That big old gate is locked. No one else is due home until tomorrow. I am alone.

The crunch of feet on gravel is a light echo that seeps in through the bathroom window and makes me go wild with fear. I crawl on my belly into the living room—there are only three rooms in this cabin—and I grab the pistol that someone's old boyfriend has given us for protection. The shotgun is in the bathroom. I have already used that once to save a woman who was on the verge of being raped, and when her attacker heard me drop the shells into the chamber he froze, and she leapt past me and into safety like a little baby rabbit. I also know how to use the pistol but tonight I'd really rather shoot at empty beer cans and not people.

The sound of crunching gravel gets closer and closer and then I see the door begin to open and I have the gun in my hand and drop to the floor. When I roll onto my hips, I have the pistol cradled just like those babes in *Charlie's Angels*. My left hand is holding my right wrist and I am ready to shoot. I'll even shoot Jesus if I have to.

"Hey," says a woman's voice as she spies the weapon. "It's me, Naomi."

"Shit, I thought you were Jesus."

My heart is like a rocket that is just a second or two from takeoff. Sweat is running down my back, my legs are shaking, fingers twitching, and my head is bobbing like it's being pulled on a string. I have the safety off and I am ready to shoot. I am overcome with the stiff feel of adrenaline and it will take a week for the muscles in my legs to fall back into place.

The woman at the door is just Naomi waltzing through the early evening looking for a canyon fire and some friendly conversation and I am poised to shoot her. We laugh, but just a little, and I ask her to maybe call the next time. Just in case, you know, Jesus might be visiting.

Later, my police friends trace the license plate of the car at the gate for me, and I am relieved to know that not only does Jesus drive a Thunderbird, he also lives in a crappy apartment complex down in the valley.

Go figure.

Jesus in an apartment.

Just when you think you know everything.

Even Now

I was so young when all those babies died.

I didn't know a damn thing about love and holding your feverish baby daughter in your arms at 3:25 a.m. or giving up the job you love so you can stay home and teach your son how to read and bake cookies that taste like burnt chocolate.

I didn't know about the anguish of leaving, even for a quick run to the grocery store. The idea of losing something that came from inside of you, that had the fabric of your heart and skin and soul was as foreign to me as the shores of lusty Cuba.

I was responding to one of those quiet emergency fire calls where everyone hurries but there really isn't anything to do. There wasn't a real fire. The whole damn thing was a fluke. Little angels coming down from heaven, some fools believe, to put a hand over the top of the stovepipe so everyone dies from poisoned air.

It was a long drive from my cabin home to this fire-call site, up the side of the river, across the mouth of the canyon and into the flat growing country that supported farmers and people who loved to live away from stoplights. My job as a newspaper reporter took me everywhere, at any time, almost all of the time. I was always on call, always ready for the next tragedy—or so I thought.

It was easy to find the house where the dispatcher had sent me because of all the fire trucks that were lined up in front of it, and then when I stepped from the warmth of my car and into the early-morning mountain air—those body bags, one, two, three, four—lined up like rows of rising carrots greeted me like a slap across my face.

Four children. Someone's babies. One maybe just barely into his teens and the parents away for the first time ever—to celebrate an anniversary.

Their plane had not even touched down at the edge of the ocean and someone had to meet them at the airport and tell them all but one of their children were dead.

Dead.

That's the scene I imagine while I am driving with the window open and my coffee cup steaming in the freezing air. The mother, falling back in disbelief, and the father, a silent stone, and all those people watching and saying, *"Oh my God,"* and their endless ride back home. Even then there was no understanding the horror of something like this. Even now.

I was nervous when I arrived and who wouldn't be. Me—a tall, young reporter with her notebook and a heart pounding like a bad engine. Wondering, as I walked from the car, past the ambulances and toward the door, what I would ask, what I would see, and least of all what I would write.

Something caused me to look up and a kind woman, a friend, a neighbor, the lady from their church told me, "Yes, you can come in, it's okay." There was a wisp of smoke, as thick as half a cigarette moving like a prayer from the silver chimney top. A killer. The killer. It seemed impossible that the body bags I walked past, shiny and black, were filled with the hopes of hearts that fluttered away just hours ago.

The kitchen was a buzz of women. Aprons flying. Food stacked upon food. Windows cracked, not just for the heat, I think, but to be sure there was air, fresh air. The women were matter-of-fact, talking about the church service, who was going to the airport, who would take the first shift so no one would be alone.

Jesus, I said to myself. It was a prayer. A curse. Something to say so I would not lose control. I kept imagining those children dying. One by one their heads would slump and then the dreadful silence and the night air finally lifting and the women who discovered them opening first one door and then the next and then, just like that, nothing is ever the same again.

The police chief in charge was the big burly guy who liked me. He told me what I needed to know and then he told me what I can never forget.

"The one boy, I think he knew," sighed the officer, talking wildly, arms flying like spinning saucers to keep himself from crying. "He was coming out of the bed like he knew something was wrong but, well, hell, I guess he couldn't make it. None of them could make it. The others were just there. You know, sleeping. I don't think they knew a thing. Just sleeping. Just sleeping."

"Would it hurt?" I ask. "Would they feel anything?"

"Nah. That's the good thing, if you know what I mean. It was like a dream, I think. Hard to breathe but they wouldn't realize what was really happening."

"Well, that's something."

"Well, it's something but hell, this is about the worst thing I've ever seen around here."

There were chalk marks in all the bedrooms where they had discovered them. Outlines of tiny bodies. A leg here. A head turned sideways. Arms reaching. When I saw the first one my stomach rose to my throat and I could have reached inside my mouth and felt it. "Oh my God."

The body outlines were so tiny. If I would have been alone I would have pushed my hand inside each white circle. Feeling for what? A spot of warmth? A missing leg? The last breath of a baby's soul? I don't know. It's just what I thought about. What I remember now.

It didn't take long to get what I need to write my story. To look around and see the socks on the floor, the pizza pan in the kitchen sink, the notes mom had left on the refrigerator door, all the bikes lined up in the driveway.

It was almost impossible to leave the house. I wanted to bake a cake with the women in the kitchen, or wash out the bathtub, or hell, I don't know, sit in the backyard and watch all the new stars float toward the tip of Mount Timpanogos, looming there in the distance. A simple news story was not going to cut it, but that's all I could do.

Winding back down the canyon highway, I cried. I knew the dead babies were dancing in the heaven they all believed in, and the parents had their faith, but I cried for something that I must have been nudging closer to each day without knowing it. It was an awful ache, just a sample of greater pain really, that swelled from a place that maybe never existed inside of me before that day. A place reserved, I think, for mothers and others who have felt the depths of love and loss and sacrifice.

Weeks later, when I heard the coyotes wail late at night from my canyon cabin, I wondered if it really wasn't that mother pouring out her grief into the same air that had claimed her precious souls. I bet it was. I am a mother now and I know it.

For years and years as I passed by that tall, brown house where I walked past the body bags and saw the chalk marks in the bedroom with the plaid bedspreads and baseball bats, I had to practice not crying.

Many, many times I did cry but I knew I had to try to forget about it all. But, I never could. I remember it now and when I am home alone and the phone rings and it is the school nurse or a strange voice asking who I am, I sometimes flip back through the pages of my mind and all I can say over and over again is just, "*Oh my God.*"

Turquoise Ring

The first time Ray would not look at me.

He came in through the restaurant's dark front door like a shifting shadow and slipped into the seat, *his seat*, at the far end of the bar. I moved from beer to coffee cup to beer until I reached him and said, "Hello."

Right away I could tell he must have had a stroke. The left side of his face would not work. It was frozen as solid as the Provo River in late January and he immediately moved his hand to cover his eye, his cheek, and any piece of flesh that he could reach with his gnarly short fingers.

"New?" he asked. It was a question that was laced with spit and more than a slur.

"Yep," I answered. "My name is Kris and all these crazy people I work with already told me your name is Ray."

He smiled. Just a half smile but it was a smile, even if he was looking past my shoulder, out the wide window, and into a clump of trees that blocked the view of the mountains just beyond the river.

"Nice to meet you," he answered and slapped the counter with his right hand.

I already knew that gesture meant he wanted his coffee. From the fresh pot, with a little cream and plenty of napkins.

The first-shift steel mill crowd came in then and Ray left in a flash but not before I noticed that he had on a beautiful silver and turquoise ring. I didn't say anything about it. It was our first date. He was shy. I had twelve cowboys and those steelworkers waiting for me. Tips were my life.

The next time Ray came in, which was the next night I worked as a waitress/barmaid, I watched him for a while when he wasn't looking. I didn't know anything about him except that he wore an amazing ring and that he was embarrassed by what had happened to his body. No one seemed to know much about him—where he came from, what he did, how he had even discovered this little joint in the middle of nowhere.

He was a short man, probably about sixty-five years old and even by the look in his fine, bright-blue right eye—the good eye as he would have called it—I could tell he was sad. I imagined him, from just this second meeting, going home each night to some little side street apartment down in the valley and watching television until he nodded off and eventually walking alone down the short hall to his single bed.

Even now I believe that everything I thought about Ray was real. He had two shirts. One plaid and the other more plaid. His shoes were simple, worn-out, brown work boots. He walked with a shuffle and seemed to slide into his seat like a cute little snake so that no one would see him dragging his bad leg. His dark hair, what was left of it, was tinged with clumps of gray and from that very first afternoon I always wanted to hug him.

In my world hugging was supposed to take care of just about everything from a broken foot to a damaged heart and I think I was born with a little tactile feeler implanted just behind my eyes that led me to people like Ray. Just a hug. That would have made him smile without his hand in front of his face and his eyes planted down, always down.

Gradually, Ray and I developed one of those interesting and comforting waitress-customer relationships. He knew that I was a struggling writer and needed to work two jobs. I told him about my newspaper stories in between customers and I always told him how much I loved his ring. He told me—what? How it was going to snow next Tuesday and that we were in for a tough winter. Not much but just enough to keep us going.

From the very beginning, probably because I had once worked in a hospital coffee shop where customers were often dripping blood, I remembered to give him extra napkins. This may seem like a simple gesture but I thought Ray was going to cry each time I did this. Sometimes he was so embarrassed he actually jammed the wet napkins into his pocket so I wouldn't have to see or touch them.

Ray could not drink his java or move his mouth without having coffee, saliva, or whatever else might be in there slip out. I am certain that's why he never ate anything in front of me, that's why he rarely had more than two cups of coffee, that's why he always sat at the far edge of the bar, in the dark corner, away from lights, people, the bathroom doors.

"Ray, baby," I would say when he slithered to his seat. "Get in here."

"Did you miss me?"

"Were you gone? I thought you were in the restroom for two days."

"I was, but I was in the women's restroom; I was waiting for you."

Okay. We flirted a little bit. Just wild banter and the kind of talk that makes people feel as if they really know each other. Often I mentioned his ring and after months and months he let me touch his hand to look at it closely. It wasn't a hug but what the hell, it was sure something.

It was not perfect turquoise but a rugged stone that was laced with dark veins and shaped in an uneven oval. Around the edge, from base to top, an artist had wound a snake of silver. I imagined a jewelry artist doing this, tucked away inside of a small studio, turning the silver and stone into this piece of beautiful magic.

"Oh, Ray," I gushed, "this ring is beautiful. Where did you get it?"

"I visited my daughter once in Arizona and I bought it from this man on the highway."

I was shocked. A daughter! A trip to Arizona! My fingers may have trembled a bit before he moved his hand back to the comforting warmth of his coffee cup. He had just told me more in the last two minutes than in the past twelve months.

"It's the most beautiful ring I've ever seen, Ray."

My writer's mind went crazy then and I imagined all sorts of wild things. His wife left him. He never married. He only saw his daughter once and this ring was all he had to remind himself of his past.

Maybe every thought was true. Maybe not. But I think so, even now, dozens of years later. Ray was a sad, lost, and lonely soul who touched the world through the edge of his cup of Joe.

I must have worked at The Chalet a good fifteen months and for fifteen months Ray was always there. We talked, laughed, he was my friend and I like to think he thought of me the same way. We never exchanged a harsh word and there were always more than enough napkins for his chin.

19

It was comforting for a young, struggling, writer-woman like me to know a friendly face waited at the end of my murder trials, obituary notices, and city council meetings. I probably let out a sigh each time I saw him. All of my own anguish and loneliness melted away in the shadow of his simple presence. I needed a hug just as much as he looked like he needed a hug.

I switched newspaper jobs, finally, and had to move down into the valley myself. It was time to become a customer at The Chalet and out of all my regular fans and friends I struggled for days with how to tell Ray that I was no longer going to be there every night.

Someone else must have told him because the last week or so before I left, he came in only once. I didn't know what to say but was sadly glad that it was busy when he came in.

"Ray …," I tried to say that last day but he put his hand up and simply shook his head from side to side. I wanted to tell him how much he meant to me, how I loved to turn and then look back and see that he had appeared, like magic, in his special seat. "Your good eye," I would tell him, "it's the kindest eye I have ever seen."

When I went back to clean up his coffee cup, the puddles of milk, the drips from his chin, I found a tiny ring box placed where he usually put my fifty-cent tip.

When I opened up the box, inside was a turquoise ring, almost like his ring. Instead of a snake there was a feather, a delicate symbol, I suppose, of all our time together. It fit perfectly and when I placed it onto my finger, it felt like a hug.

Could he have driven to Arizona? Stopped at every roadside jewelry vendor? Called his lost-again daughter and asked for help? How did he know my ring size?

I never saw Ray again. Not once. But I think about him all the time and I have the ring and I have this story and a memory of my friend in the corner, his heart beating, a stifled laugh, and fingers as light as a feather dancing against the side of my arm.

The Mothers in Bosnia

It was their eyes.

I'm in an Air Force cargo plane, the one so gigantic you can drive a tractor into the belly, and we are delivering flour to the starving residents of Sarajevo.

Already, after just one flight in and out of this war-torn city, I think I should not be here. I should be home playing cards with my son and watching *Sesame Street* with my daughter instead of flying into a war zone. What the hell is wrong with me?

There is a good chance our plane will be shot down and hours after this thought first enters my mind someone does shoot at us. But that is after I see their eyes, these mothers who are trying to get someone to help them, to listen to them, to save their own babies.

The women were not scheduled to fly back to Croatia with us. I am with a group of Air Force reservists and we are shuttling flour and people in between these two tiny, ravaged countries. We pick up flour at the bullet-riddled airport in Split, along the Adriatic Sea, and then make a run for Sarajevo, which looks like a sandbagged slice of hell.

The first time I run into the airport past all the tiny, dark-haired men, I am treated like a blonde queen. Men with rifles and revolvers tucked into their belts reach out to run their hands along the edges of my hair, down my back, across the top of my rear end. They allow me to pass through customs first and they give me a special stamp on my passport that other people have to pay for because this country—it no longer exists. At five feet ten inches, I am a giant of a woman to them, and they are looking through my clothes and running their hands over every inch of my body without actually touching me.

This doesn't bother me. What bothers me are the bullet holes in the walls above the spot where I sip coffee as strong as old tar. What bothers me is that even in a moment of lust their eyes are dark and sad and weeping. What bothers me is that many of these people will be dead by the time I am home drinking a glass of wine and taking a hot bath.

The world here is so changed that there are no birds flying through the sky. No fires coming from the few chimneys that remain standing. When we land, people run in a jagged line in case there is a sniper hiding out at the edge of the airfield. Not one breath is taken for granted.

This is not the Sarajevo I remember from watching the Olympics when I was a little girl. I remember beautiful snowcapped mountains and smiling people who wore wool hats and always seemed to be drinking something with steam coming out of it. I remember gorgeous figure skaters and a land that reminded me of those fairy-tale books my mother always read to me.

What I see is a bleak landscape that seems to be dying as I watch it. Trees with the tops blown off. Brown grass singed with rings of black fire. Homes that have collapsed and turned into piles of rubble. No people. No cars on the gravel highways. The sky is even a listless shade of blue that seems to fade as I glide through a few brave clouds.

When we land, after a series of evasive maneuvers to throw off whoever might have us in their gun sights, the sense of danger does not evaporate.

"If you leave this plane we will not help you," the commander of the mission tells us. "Stay away from the back of the plane. This is a war zone."

We are wearing heavy flak jackets and around our necks little chains dangle that will help our loved ones identify our bullet-riddled bodies. It is so hard for me to follow directions. It goes against my very nature. If they say don't look over there I immediately want to rush to the corner with my notepad and take a peek.

I can't help myself. Something is wrong with me. When they unload the flour, I race to the back of the plane and show the enemy my large head. I step out onto the edge of the loading dock so I am actually out of the airplane. I want to see what it's like to take a breath of air in a sea of hate.

Someone grabs me. The man who has his arm on the seams of my flak jacket is not smiling and I am back in the plane in less than one minute. While I wait for the back end to come up I see three figures run for the ramp of our airplane. They are moving like spring lightning, holding nothing, and when they get close I see that they are women.

When they get to the belly of the plane some of the soldiers haul them inside and usher them to the little web seats welded into the side of the airplane. The women look as if they could be heading off to pick up their kids from school. They have on light jackets, boots, jeans that are well worn.

"Who are they?" I ask one of the soldiers.

"I guess they are nurses who are trying to get some more help," he tells me, yelling through the constant hum of the vibrating metal that surrounds us. "They need medicine, all kinds of stuff, and they are trying to get some more people to donate."

"Do they speak English?"

The soldier moves his head back and forth.

I know these women are not just nurses. They are all wearing wedding bands and they are mothers. I know this without speaking to them and I look each one of them in the eye and smile. Mothers know many, many things.

I am quickly caught up interviewing a Spanish peacekeeping soldier who has just seen the dead bodies of three children. He speaks perfect English, has beautiful dark eyes, hair that hangs in graceful waves across his forehead, and he is also wearing a wedding ring.

"The mother was working in the garden," he tells me as quietly as he can so I have to lean in, my ear to his mouth, to hear this horrid story above the rumbling in the airplane. The soldier stops every few seconds to rub his eyes, to try to stay composed. "There were three shots. One. Two. Three. Before she could move—all three of her children were shot. Right in front of her."

My heart is pounding as fast as the engine of this huge plane. When he describes these murders I can see everything in my mind without closing my eyes. Perhaps it is one of those little villages we flew over just twenty minutes ago. The mother is bent over her wooden rake, pulling at the earth while the children run through the rows of beets and step on the weeds. They laugh. They complain. They want to escape down the hill and play in the stream. The mother admonishes them. She never stops working. Everyone is hungry. They are always hungry.

"I saw the bodies, lying there, still warm," he tells me. "I can never forget this. Never."

I reach out to touch this man who I will probably never see again. I place my hand over the top of his and ask him if he has children. There are long creases at the edge of his eyes that disappear into the sides of his black hair. I wonder if these are new lines and if he was a young man when he left for this horrid mission.

"Yes," he says. "I have not seen them in a long time. I am going home."

My babies. My babies. I cannot stop thinking about my babies and I am hating myself for being in this fucking airplane and not at home. But I am a writing soldier. There are stories to tell. My hand is an endless wave. I write down every word.

"Do you have to come back?"

"Oh, yes." The soldier nods. "This is my job. I will be back."

It is my job to tell his story, to tell all the stories I can manage to hear during a few days in the heart of the war. I convince myself of this as I close my eyes and feel what must only be a fraction of the pain this man is now feeling.

Then I open my eyes, look up, and I also want to tell the stories of these women, sitting across from me but I feel so damn helpless. When my lunch is handed to me I can think of nothing but to give my food to these people. I let the man eat my sandwich and I scrounge through my camera bag to get candy and gum and crackers for the women who are eating someone else's lunch.

When I make my way across the plane, they all smile at me, like they have been waiting for me to wake up and get over there. I am the only woman they see on this airplane and there is always a web of sisterhood that joins women together, even here while people are dying directly below us, when we cannot speak the same language, when our worlds are so far apart, we are sisters, always sisters.

I want to know if they have babies. Are their husbands alive? When will they get back to Bosnia? Are their homes still standing? Did their mothers die in the last bombing? What about older brothers? Which sides are they fighting on? What supplies do they need? When was the last time they made love? But there is not much time.

"Babies?" I ask, pointing to my own uterus, and making believe I am holding a baby.

They all nod. They are not carrying wallets. There are no photos, but I can see their babies in my mind's eye. Dark hair. One with blue eyes. Two are girls. These women and their children are all friends. Before all of this the children played in the park while the mothers sat outside on the concrete sidewalk and drank warm glasses of tart wine.

My God. Where are the babies now? I can't ask this. I can't really ask anything. I unload my pockets and give them everything I can think of. They take it all and smile and look into my eyes to see what they can of my life. One of them slides over so our hips are touching and she grabs onto the edge of my coat. With that one swift gesture she is saying thank you, help us, save us, we are so tired and frightened. I want to take them all with me but they will never leave without their babies—they are mothers, nurses, saviors.

When they get off the plane, I hug each one of them. They are skin and bones and they are in a big hurry. They hug me back. One touches me on the face and smiles and then they run as fast as they can into a crowd of soldiers from where? Russia, maybe. They are gone. When I lift my head and look across the sea of madness, past the guns and the tanks, past the rolling airplanes filled with bombs, they have vanished.

No one can hear me sob because the plane is so damn loud. It is also windy so my tears fly away before they actually form. I feel as if someone has a hand around my heart. It aches. I am emotionally bruised and have never felt so helpless.

The peacekeeping soldier also gets off. He thanks me and runs toward another airplane. He will be home in a day. The women may never be home again.

By midnight I am sitting in a cafeteria, looking for a pilot who will let me sleep in his room while he is flying an all-night mission. There is no place else for me to stay on this air base and I am so tired I can barely walk. When I call my story into the newspaper, my old journalism professor who works there answers the phone and in astonishment says, "My God, you are something."

I do not want to astonish. What I want to be is home. I want everyone to be home. I want those women to fly back into Sarajevo with a plane full of food and medical supplies and a secret potion for peace. I want to climb into my own bed just after hearing the quiet sighs of my two children who have come to kiss me and fallen asleep in my arms.

It will be days before I fly back into my calm, safe American life. I will first fly to some tiny islands and then greet soldiers who are flying off to another war in Turkey and then I will come home and bake cookies for school, clean the bathrooms, and hang the sheets out on the backyard line. I will be myself and never again the same.

Sometimes, when I scan the newspapers or the television news, I watch for those women. When I think I can't make it until Friday or when I think my life is hard I remember them—their sad eyes, the fingers on my heart. I will never know what happened to them.

But I buried their smiles, the few moments we shared, the bonds of the moment—a meeting of chance—inside of my heart. They are safe there, in a warm cavern where everything and everyone is always beautiful and I pray for them with such passion that I am exhausted all these years later each time I wave them into the forefront of my mind.

Wong's Silver Spur, Dead Deer, and the Dance-Floor Stabbing

Carolyn is so mortified I think she is about to drop to the floor and vanish into the hotel lobby. We have answered the long-awaited knock at the door. Our dates have arrived.

She gets Don. He's a groovy accountant who is madly in love with her but she is engaged to marry Mr. Steve who is studying entomology in California. Carolyn and Don are pals but he is clearly in love with her. His eyes follow her every move and he touches her arm, her hand, any piece of her whenever he gets close enough to touch skin.

Don looks like just the kinda guy he is. A Montana boy who went to college, got a great job with the government, and can afford new Ropers and one of those wide belts with a brass buckle. He's smart, kind, genuinely nice and it looks like he is desperately trying not to fall to his knees and kiss Carolyn's little feet.

Carolyn is my pal, my girlfriend, my confidante, the flip of my flop, my bosom buddy. We are also madly in love with each other as best friends are and so naughty together that I would have to kill you if I told you everything. When we are not together we are constantly on the phone planning our next rendezvous. In this Western wilderness, finding a female soul mate is the last drop of fresh water that keeps us alive and we don't know it yet but tonight will be the night to beat all nights.

My date is, well, let's call him Larry. He looks like a Larry. Remember that dating game we played when the boys were shooting cap guns at each other, where the loser had to go out with Poindexter? That's Larry. He has on big black glasses that hang so low on his nose there is no way in hell he could see out of them. His pants are too short. He has on a red plaid polyester shirt that has white snaps on it. His shoes are oxfords. Honest to God. Every word of this is true. He is alive and standing there with his hands hanging down past his knees and his shoulders rounded, and he is trying to remember how to speak English.

Carolyn, for the first time since I have known her, is struck dumb. I suck it in like a big girl, step forward and say, "Hi, Larry, thanks for coming." The night is about to begin.

Waiting for us is Don's big honkin' pickup truck. Carolyn is from Berkeley, California. She is so hip that when she walks the word cool flies off her skin. She's granola and bell-bottoms and long hair and invisible cosmetics that make her smell like a June rainstorm. I'm from Wisconsin, so not much fazes me. My family was always just an inch from vulgar. We talked dirty, yelled, and then kissed like crazy. On special holidays, my father would open the back door and shoot one of his weapons into the dark night air, scaring the living hell out of the neighbors who never did get used to it. Montana looks as if it's far from Wisconsin on the maps but it's really not far at all.

We have both worn our new coats, mine is leather and Carolyn's is a fashionable camel hair from Seattle. When Carolyn turns to flip her coat behind her so we can all get into the truck, she sees the dead deer head looking at her from the back of the truck cab.

"What the hell! What is that thing?""

"It's a deer."

"What the hell is it doing back there?"

"Nothing," explains Larry. "It's dead."

I am trying so hard not to laugh because I know if I do I will piss in my pants before the night gets cranked up—not that anyone would even notice. The four of us are crammed into the pickup truck like little sausages wrapped in plastic and Carolyn is trying to whisper something like "Help me" in my ear.

"We just shot 'um and we didn't want to be late."

"Nice horns," I offer. "It'll keep out in this cold mountain air for months if you don't have a freezer."

I can tell Larry likes me. He pushes up his glasses and says, "Yup."

Dinner is unmemorable. Nobody spilled anything. We had, of course—meat, potatoes, and two peas and we found out about the big hunt and dragging the buck to the truck. Carolyn kept mouthing, "I'm so sorry," any time one of the men turned their heads.

Well, hell, I really didn't care. It was already better than the guy in Havre who drove me around with a gun in his hand all night. Besides that, we were going dancing and I had already found out the hard way that women in Montana do not dance together. They do in Wisconsin. They do in Minnesota. They do in California. But never, ever, ever never in Montana.

This lesson I learned the hard way when my pal Char came to visit and we went to the local bar and danced together like we had since high school and some guys laughed at us and we got into a fight. We ran out the door after I backed up toward the stage and the microphone fell into the lead singer's mouth. Char and I ran like hell but first we grabbed our beers off the table and then drank them as we walked home through the dark alley.

So I have not been dancing in a while and I love to dance and the boys have a real treat planned for us. They are taking us to Wong's Silver Spur.

"What are the chances that someone from China would open up a cowboy bar in Montana?" Carolyn asks as we amble along with the rolling deer head behind us. From the front I imagine this head looks like a strange fifth passenger except here no one would really say anything about it.

"This place has been here a while and it's the hottest joint in town," Don informs us.

"Do they have a real band?" I ask.

"Yea and it gets wild on the weekends."

Oh goodie. The parking lot is jammed and Carolyn is looking and looking and can't believe that Wong's is located inside of a tin Quonset hut. This realization brings so many sideways glances from Carolyn that I think her eyes are going to roll out of her head at an angle. We decide to leave our beautiful coats in the car.

In my world Quonset huts are places to park tractors and where you keep the summer seed and where thousands of Japanese-Americans were forced to live during the Second World War. It's not someplace you would think of to go and dance and drink large quantities of liquor.

The place is absolutely packed. It feels like the entire building is swaying, and Don and Larry rush to get us a tray of beers while Carolyn and I clutch each other and laugh and say things like, "This is the funniest night" and "Do you think Larry has ever had a date before?" We immediately rule out the idea of having group sex.

Larry will not dance. He has a hard time walking, he tells me. Carolyn and Don disappear for one, two, and almost three beers. This makes Larry loosen up just a bit. He unbuttons the top of his shirt. I notice his oxford's moving just an inch or so.

After Carolyn and Don finally return, Don gets me on the dance floor and I am mesmerized by the variety of people who are in Wong's. Cowboys and a few guys in shirts with ties hanging to their waists and women with that hairdo that I have come to call the Wyoming where the hair is short in front and really long in back. "What's with that?" Carolyn always says. "It's like they got scared when they got to cutting the back."

We are cooking after what I think is about a six-pack each. The noise and yelling and people screaming for drinks have reached a fascinating level. No one can really talk and then Larry decides he will dance.

This is very exciting for all of us and Larry hops up and starts dancing—alone. I sneak up behind him and start dancing by myself. He is pretty much doing that brother-in-law never-learned-how-to-dance thing where you just jump from foot to foot and think about welding or some damn thing.

Larry is having a great time, and he races back to the table and grabs his drink so he can dance with his beer and not just himself. I figure I will not dance again until I move from Montana so I do the same thing.

"Hey, Larry," I yell, "I bet you never thought you'd have this much fun tonight."

"Nope, but I never thought I'd have eleven beers and get drunk either."

Larry is such a charmer. He says all the right things.

Before we know what's happening, there is some kind of commotion going on about four couples from us. It's a fight and people are screaming and other people are ignoring it and suddenly, right there by the edge of my feet, someone is being dragged off the dance floor and there is a trail of blood. People notice this red stuff and they just kick through it with their boots and shoes and sawdust and popcorn and napkins.

"A stabbing," Larry says like he just saw his ninety-fifth one of the season.

"A stabbing?"

"Happens all the time. He'll probably live. He wasn't much of a bleeder."

Well I'll be damned. No one skips a beat and there are some flashing lights outside and a few more rounds of beers and then we have to help Larry to the truck where the three of us look at each other for a minute and then decide without saying a word not to put him in the back of the truck with the dead deer.

Carolyn and I take turns standing in the shower for about a week because we smell like the inside of an ashtray and there is beer in interesting places that feels fairly alarming. While one of us is in the shower the other one lies on the bed and laughs and laughs. There is no stopping us.

It is almost time to get up when we go to bed and when we do wake up with hangovers we are still laughing and we have been laughing for the past three decades about the night of Larry and deer, pickup trucks, Wong's, and the stabbing.

Years ago, Carolyn and I did a two-week Thelma and Louise trip back through Montana. We drove around without our bras on because once we almost got fired for not wearing them to work, we kept the windows down all the time, set a new record for the number of hours people talk without stopping, and went back to Wong's.

Carolyn ordered a beer and she said it was her first one in three decades. I believed her because she moved back to California where they grow all those grapes. Wong's had not changed at all and I wondered if they had bothered to sweep the floor since the last time we had been there. I believed that if I bent down on the dance floor I would be able to see a little track of red blood leading toward the back door. I loved Wong's even more the second time.

We were the only two women in the bar, in the middle of the day, and we were dressed like people who do not live in Montana. Outside there were trucks and beat-up cars from the night before when all the drunk drivers were dragged home by friends and fellow drinkers.

We ordered a couple of beers and made eye contact with the nervous barkeep. Wong sold the joint, he told us, and I asked him if women could dance together yet in the state of Montana. "It's risky," he told us looking sideways as he backed up.

Carolyn and I laughed and I almost pissed in my pants again and then I ordered a shot of whiskey because it seemed like the perfect thing to do.

All these miles and years later there is rarely a week when I don't hear someone like Shania Twain and flash back to that glorious night when the boys and Carolyn and I kicked ass not far from the Lewis and Clark Trail, and I think about how this story has ridden with me for so long it feels like part of my left arm. It stays with me like Carolyn's smile, the touch of her fingers on my arm when we talked, twelve cups of coffee in the morning, and I know I would not be who I am just this moment if instead of all of this we had simply eaten Chinese and watched a long movie.

And Larry. Whatever in the hell do you think happened to Larry anyway?

The Backseat of the Black Ford with the Red Ashtrays

It is my turn to sit in the middle of the backseat. It is the twenty-eighth day of our cross-country family camping trip, and my sister has had her fingers slammed in the door in Oregon, my father would not let us swim in the Great Salt Lake, and after that my mother didn't speak to him for one hundred and fifty-eight miles as we passed through Nevada and into California where we stood in dumbstruck awe when we saw that my dad's old Marine buddy really did have a swimming pool in his backyard. Now I am in the middle and I hate it.

This trip is the biggest deal of our lives. It's bigger than last Christmas and my fourteenth birthday and driving around Lake Superior in six days and seeing a bear cross the highway. It's bigger than my brother Jeff telling me he learned how to smoke a pipe at YCC Camp and my father finding out he has diabetes and my grandma dying that cold morning when she was not so much older than my own mother is now.

My father is a brick mason and it seems impossible that he is not working fourteen hours a day for one whole month so he can show his family the West and see his Marine buddy from the war, George. Now I know that my parents must have saved and scrimped and what could they have given up in order to pay for this because we never had excess money. In the winters, when it was sometimes too cold to work, my father would go out hunting for rabbits or a deer that he would bring home in the dark for dinner. How could they have done this? Taken us on this trip and driven all those miles and then stayed together after the weight of everything that we have seen and experienced, and those miles when no one was allowed to speak?

We set up our little trailer on the prairie and in the forests and then in the mountains, which made my heart explode with joy. Each night while my father snored and my brothers farted, and when I heard my mother shift in that way that meant she was finally asleep, I would drag my thin sleeping bag out of the trailer and sleep on those plastic seats in that black Ford with the red ashtrays. The metal and plastic held the cold and I would shiver and shiver but even then I liked to be alone with all those thoughts that had already made me feel not like anyone else I knew. I would lie awake and look through the windshield at the stars caressing the tops of the mountains and I would compose poems and dream of cowboys and count on my fingers how many days it would be until I would be living in a spot just like this.

In the morning my mother would come and knock on the window with her boney knuckles and say, "Are you okay?" and then we would eat very quickly and I would pee in the bushes because that always seemed better than a stinking outhouse and we would work so fast to throw everything back in the trailer so we could get going and see something else, something new, everything in the whole world.

We ate sandwiches covered with wax paper and at night we cooked over the fires and a couple of times we ate in a restaurant with strict instructions not to order drinks or anything that cost more than a dime. In one swoop of extravagance, my father let us go horseback riding and I was so happy I cried into my hands as the black horse was led toward me. When we rode the horses up a steep cliff and I realized we were one step away from tumbling off the edge that exact moment is when a feeling of excitement and wonder and searching started to grow inside of me that today is as large as a small foreign car.

On this trip I learned how to whistle with both my fingers tucked under my tongue after the seventeenth day of trying. I read all my books and in my mind I wrote two novels, a book of poems and my memoirs, while we rambled from state to state and my eyes inhaled the desert sands, the ranch fences that looked like little dots that disappeared in the horizon, and all the people who rode tractors to town to buy milk and houses that had no gutters on them because of all the damned snow my father told us.

By the twenty-eighth day I had my entire life planned out. I was going to leave home the minute no one looked and come back to the West. I was going to marry a cowboy named Jack Patch and then I could be Kris Radish Patch and I would write all day and he would rope cows and then come home and kiss me while I fried up some beef.

Heading east again we have just spent the day in Jackson Hole, Wyoming. My mother has taken our photograph as we stand under the arch of elk horns, we have jumped on and off the barstools that are really saddles, and we watched a make-believe shootout where cowboys fired guns and then dropped dead on the dusty road.

I didn't care about any of that stuff. I just wanted to go sit in the mountains and write poems and imagine all the days and nights of my life that I knew would be absolutely brilliant and wonderful. But we had to drive and drive because there was no money left and our real lives were waiting for us back in Wisconsin.

Past the elk refuge I manage to turn my neck and crank around so that my hands and arms are resting on the edge of the window in this black car that is way too small for a family of six on a monthlong camping trip.

My brothers, the goobers, are picking their arms and my sister, the princess, gets to sit in the front seat beside the king and queen. None of this really matters to me because I am sifting out pieces of my heart and soul along the edge of the highway. I am leaving a trail that only I will really, honest to God, follow back to the mountains in six very long and sometimes troubling years.

My eyes are locked in an embrace with the Teton Mountains that have succeeded in seducing me. When I open up my fingers, I can feel snow from the tips of the rocks melting on them and the air is so thin that I am breathing in shallow, dangerous gulps. This could be the first moment in my life when I feel sexy. I am intoxicated, and a smell that is earthy and scented with pine rolls off my body. My hips shift and I feel an ache between my legs that is the humbling blow of love.

It is impossible for me to tear myself away from this view and everything and everyone else disappears as I memorize each profile, the glistening lakes, the way the sage reaches out to touch the edge of the asphalt like a frightened predator, and miles of fence posts standing erect in the morning sun.

When we finally turn the last corner and the mountains disappear, I have them etched into my mind so permanently, that thirty-three years later I can draw them in my sleep.

One summer, when I have already crossed more than my share of mountain peaks, I bring my own children to this very spot and their daddy scouts for snakes as we set up our backpacking tent at the edge of a lake that has a view of the mountains that I know without even opening my eyes. The kids play Indians and I fill my tin cup with wine and I sit on a log and watch as clouds cover the summit and the trees sway and then out of the corner of my eye I notice that my son and daughter are standing still and they have their arms around each other. They are not moving, they have become mountain statues and they are looking at the mountains, and I know they have fallen in love.

"What are you doing?" I ask them gently, sneaking up from behind.

When I turn, I see that their eyes are shining, and they are very serious, and that they are about to tell me something magical that will make me realize once again that there is some kind of God or Goddess and that she has wrapped us all around her slender fingers.

"We're watching the mountains," my daughter tells me.

"We have to know everything about them," her brother adds.

"It's magnificent. Just look. Can you feel it?"

"Is this where you were before, Mom?"

"Many times," I tell them.

"Right here?"

"Close to this spot. Maybe not right here but...."

"Did you leave some of your heart here, Mom? You always say things like that. Is this one of those places?"

"Yep. That's how I found my way back."

Then they do an elaborate dance and they sprinkle mist from their souls onto the bushes, they tell me, so that they can find their way back, too.

When we leave, down that same highway, I turn to look out of the back window of the van, and when I move I have a sudden vision of a fourteen-year-old girl with her black, pointy glasses,

41

plaid pedal pushers, a white sleeveless blouse, her blonde curly hair an unpredictable mess. She has her arms stretched toward the mountain peaks and she is memorizing every single thing she sees. When she catches my eye I smile, because I can see she looks like my son and has the legs and gangly arms of my daughter, and I know without asking that she has just found her way back home once again.

The Day They Sliced Me Open

I watched in astonished silence as the young doctor slipped his fingers, his wrist, what seemed like thirteen yards of his arm, into my uterus. In seconds, as long as it took me to remember the story my then-husband told about his friend, the pig farmer, doing the same thing to the hogs, the doctor's eyes went from kind, to "Oh my God," to very frightened.

"The baby's heart, it's not beating right, and he's breech."

Well, so much for planning the perfect delivery. The only class I missed during the past nine months was the class on C-section births—like that's going to happen to a big, old, corn-fed gal like me. Now I was going to be sliced open like a ripe watermelon.

By the time Andrew was discovered lying inside of me ass-backwards, I had already had it with the labor business. Who were they trying to kid? I wanted a gallon of gin, cocaine, heroin, a quarter barrel of beer. Someone had screwed up the epidural—"Too late now, honey," some old bitchy nurse bellowed across the room. I wanted to gouge out her eyes and hit her right below that one rib, where my father taught me to whack someone who messed with me.

"I've changed my mind," I tried to tell someone, anyone. "I don't want to have this baby."

Cute. Real cute. Someone must have said that but I was down in the dark trenches of hell just after that utterance, dancing with a wave of pain that made me feel like someone was trying to make me swallow my own feet, while I was baking a cake and playing tennis.

Then I was scared. More scared than I was the time that guy tried to rape me and the time that other man held me against those boxes in the bowels of the warehouse. More scared than I was the time I hung outside of the helicopter with no ropes. More scared than I was the day I got married or that time that jackass tried to break into my bedroom window.

They shouldn't leave people alone when things like this happen. I knew something terrible was going on. People were flying around me like migrating geese. I was paralyzed with fear. Then someone spoke.

"Asleep or awake?"

"What?"

"Do you want to stay awake and watch your baby being born or should we put you to sleep?"

"Can I be awake but not watch you slice me open?"

"Sure honey, we'll just tilt the mirrors."

They were lying. Who wants to watch someone cut their stomach in half? The mirrors never moved and I saw everything.

"Do you want the scar to be up and down or horizontal?"

"What?"

"Should we cut you this way or that way?"

"What's the best way?"

"Do you want to wear a bikini again?"

"Are you kidding me?"

"No."

"I'm never going out in public again."

"Well, up and down heals better. We don't slice as many muscles and things."

Things? Like my baby's feet or ears?

I gesture up and down, and then brace myself for the huge needle they will insert in a space the size of a speck of dust in the middle of my spine.

At this point I stupidly realize there is no turning back. I can barely sit up and I am so huge, really huge, sixty-five pounds more than I have ever weighed in my life, that when I swing my legs down I almost roll off the table like a beached whale.

Well, this is the frigging story of my life. Things that are supposed to be easy end up being hard. They induce my labor so it comes riding into my life like an entire army of savage men. This pain straddles me for hours and hours with such ferocity I think that someone is dancing inside of me with fifteen knives. I can feel my bones moving, muscles snapping, fibers straining, and I am desperate to ask one of the good-looking nurses if she will run off with me. I am never having sex with a man again and then they say they have to cut me open anyway. "Oops." Oops my ass.

It hurts to breathe and I wish I could look into the eyes of the man who is doing this to me. Did he get enough sleep last night? Is he an alcoholic? Where did he go to medical school? One part of me can't even believe I am here, in the operating room, about to have a baby, and the other part of me, well hell, the other part of me feels the same way.

When I was a young girl, just minutes ago it seems, I was fascinated by the Civil War. I loved the stories about the women who dressed up like men to save the day, and other stories about women who worked in the field hospitals and helped saw off limbs until they were piled as high as the tent flaps. This image seeps through my weary mind as I lie down and people begin poking me below my neck to see if I have become temporarily paralyzed.

I know this baby has to come out but what a way to do it. I can't help it. I look when the doctor holds up the knife. It's just like in the movies, only worse because it's real. I try to raise my hands to stop him, I try to scream, I try to run into the forest, but there is only one tiny part of my body that I can control and it is my left eyelid.

My then-husband is right there having all the fun. I hate his guts. He has on a gown and a mask, and his hands are on the side of my head. He's watching everything and I can't believe he has not fainted. I don't remember a thing he said but I did tell him many, many times that we will never have sex again. "Lay it up here," I want to say. "We'll have him slice it off."

Everything happened fast once the last male doctor I will ever allow in my life cuts me, and in that instant, when they peeled back all the layers of my skin and muscle and exposed my womb to the cold air, the millions of sit-ups, the hundreds of miles of hiking, the jogging, the leg lifts—it all perished and I became a young woman with a long scar and a roll of fat a duck could hide inside of, and oh my God, *a baby*.

"It's a boy."

I saw him, full of blood, and as big as a small car, and they took him away and I couldn't move, which pissed me off. I was strapped to the bed and my hands were at my sides and I couldn't move.

They brought him back as fast as they could with his cleared lungs, screaming like a fast-moving train, but I could not touch him because my hands were suddenly made of evaporating rubber. But I called out his name. "Andrew," I said, sobbing. "Andrew, Mom is here."

And it was a miracle. He stopped crying and he looked right at me and he was my baby and he knew me. That was enough. "Shoot me," I said to someone. "I can die a happy woman."

My then-husband got to hold him while they wheeled me into a recovery room and left me there all by myself again. I lied and told the baby's daddy, "Go, make the calls, I'll be fine." He left, never touching the ground, this happy man with a son, and when he left I cried in astonishment and relief until someone came in to dim the lights and I dreamt about large breasts, waterfalls in the middle of cities, and men who sang instead of talked.

That was the beginning of everything. There would be more waiting and more sacrifices than can ever be measured and a scar that I can touch and that still throbs whenever I wear clothes with elastic—which is pretty much all the time. Mostly, though, there is Andrew, who hears my voice and every single time turns his head because he knows me. I am his mother.

Spaghetti Dinner

The police radio blared out information about the accident like a husky bartender bellowing for the last call. It didn't sound good and from my little cub reporter's desk I tried everything to make myself look like a notepad, a desk drawer, a broken chair—anything but a reporter.

"Radish," she yelled, this editor who had decided the moment she saw me that I was nothing more than a piece of walking dead meat. "Get up here."

Later in my life, this woman became my friend when she was in a relationship with another friend of mine. Then we became sort-of-colleagues at a university where we both tried to teach children how to write. But this day she was the queen and I was a young thing who should never have left her mother.

I was a summer journalism intern at a daily newspaper back when there were real reporters and editors who barked and didn't talk and where it was make-it-or-break-it for young reporter wannabes. I was about to have my feet held to the fire by a cranky editor.

"Did you bring your car today?"

"Yes."

"Good. There's some kind of accident going on over in New Berlin. Sounds like a fatality. Go cover the story."

My mind was exploding. I could hardly stand I was so frightened but I had to move so I could catch up with my stomach.

"Photographer?" I asked trying to sound like I knew at least one thing. Real reporters always left the office with a photographer.

"Later."

It wasn't far to New Berlin and the scene of the accident but how I got there I will never recall. A fatality. A death. My first real accident story. Scared as hell. Wondering why I didn't go to that other school and become a psychologist. Wondering why I am not hanging out in the Student Union with all my friends. Wondering how I can keep from vomiting if it's as bad as it sounds.

Back at the office, they are all laughing. I didn't know this then, and still don't care, but they are thinking I am a wimp because they don't know me. This is something they do for all the little cubbies. Scare the living hell out of them. Send them out alone. Wait for something particularly grizzly. Let them drop to the earth and cry for help. They will be sorry.

The dump truck is still making that terrible, "Watch it I'm backing up" sound when I pull into the parking lot. I recognize the coroner right away and know I'm in for it. This guy is notorious for hanging out at death scenes. He's a terrific coroner, loves his work, very helpful, absolutely enjoys the gory details. Blood and guts is his business and today he is a very happy man.

He looked a little bit like someone who should be named Boris. Bushy eyebrows, thinning dark hair, eyeballs that seem to have been jolted loose from their sockets, fingers always moving like they are trying to dry themselves, a frayed white shirt and a tie that must have drifted off the Titanic. He was perfect for his deathly job and he loved to talk with reporters.

Mr. Coroner was glad to oblige my requests for information. His report wasn't finished, but he could show me around. Tell me what happened. Explain what the last moments of someone's life must have been like.

"Well, I think he had a heart attack because no one could just slip, well maybe, but I'm thinking that's what happened," he tells me as we walk toward the truck.

"Who was it?"

"I'll tell you but you can't print it until we notify his relatives."

"They don't know yet?"

"It just happened. We have to find them."

Already I'm worried about my deadline. My reporter's genes are smashing around inside my chest and I want to run to a phone.

"His name was Arnold Dexheimer."

Arnold Dexheimer. Arnold Dexheimer. Arnold Dexheimer. He will never know that I can never forget him, that for the next thirty years he will always be in my mind, that every police call, every death scene, every siren will make his name rise inside of me like a full moon.

Arnold fell under the dump truck and the driver did not know it. While the driver was dropping his load, the long steel shafts under the truck went over and over Arnold's body.

"It wasn't pretty," says the coroner.

Then he stops for just a second, looks at me closely, and asks, "Do you want to see it?"

It? What could that be? I am trying to imagine who has to tell his wife and his children. Wondering how I am going to get his name in time for the deadline. Thinking about what it would be like to waitress the rest of my life after I drop out of journalism school.

"Okay," I respond slowly.

The coroner walks me over to the back end of the truck, which by the way, is finally silent. He bends down. I bend down. He scoots toward the wheels, I scoot. Then he points. I look.

"See it?"

I peer into the dark space and I see stuff hanging from the bottom of the truck. There are pieces of flesh and blood and other things that I may have once studied in a science class.

"Oh, yep, I see what happened."

Ironically, none of this makes me sick to my stomach. It is because, I know now, that I never saw Arnold before this happened, when he was alive and a construction worker and a man, a real man. I was thinking, even at that early moment, like a reporter. But it was just for a short time because my quest to meld the facts with the human angle was walking right behind me.

Rushing back to the office, waiting for the coroner's cause of death, I still do not get sick. But I think about his family. This part I will never get over. Never ever. The wife opening the door and the man standing there with his hard hat in his hands, and then that awkward moment when she wants to drop to the floor and he wants to catch her, and they stand there, both of them, waving like little flags until one moves just a little bit, and then the grieving begins.

After the deadline, still not knowing that this was my test, I am resting my head on my typewriter when John, one notch ahead of me on the reporter's totem pole, comes up to me, smirking, thinking he is going to get me and says, "Hey, how about going to lunch with us right now?"

I am not hungry. I may never be hungry again but I look into his eyes and I know that I cannot let this pass. He is grinning and pompous and eager to move up the pole.

"Sure," I say, jumping to my feet, "as long as we go someplace that has spaghetti."

The newsroom goes silent. Even John, who usually talks nonstop, is speechless. All the reporters who have been listening turn away. John walks in a circle around my desk and I know I have him.

Lunch I can't remember. The story headline I can't remember, but Arnold's name and that day and the realization of what I had to do, what I was becoming, who I would be, have always stayed inside of me.

Salt and Pepper

When Mike, who was a woman, hired me for my first real job, I thought she had made a mistake.

"Me?" I asked her, flabbergasted that something good had happened in my fourteen-year-old life. "You hired me?"

Mike was tall and when she walked she looked like a swaying willow that was moving to an unspoken rhythm. She was not an attractive woman in the popular sense of the word—you know one of those 1960s babes who used hairspray, wore nylons, and sat with their legs crossed—but I always thought she was one of the most-beautiful women I have ever known. She emitted a sense of kindness, and the quiet way she moved and talked and loved to touch other people's arms, hands, shoulders was a gorgeous gesture that made her seem incredibly attractive—and that little spot just below their eyes.

Her long fingers were constantly working at something, car keys, someone's elbow, plastic lace, anything she could get her hands on. Mike never raised her voice and when I was around her I felt, well, wonderful and secure and full of self-confidence. What a joy for a fourteen-year-old who had a hard time walking and breathing at the same time.

"Kris, you can do this. I really wanted you to have the job and it's yours."

"Are you sure?"

"Of course I'm sure. Look at you. This is perfect for you and you are going to do great."

At this tender age I had already barreled into so much rejection that I was all but certain someone with straight blonde hair, clothes that never wrinkled, and long fingernails would get the job. I remember jumping into the air out on the lawn where I had been interviewed when I floated to the car to tell my mother about the job.

It was a Girl Scout camp job. My first of many camp jobs and it also happened to be the hottest summer in the recorded history of the world. People were frying eggs on the roads and grown men were fainting and the air had the perpetual smell of burnt rubber and charred skin.

I was in charge of food distribution and pretty much anything else Mike decided I could handle. I walked from one edge of the camp to the next to find all the poison ivy. I hauled buckets. I packed lettuce into plastic bags, gave little girls outhouse cleaning lessons, and passed out lots of salt pills. I directed the delivery trucks and helped the handyman organize tent poles. I lifted boxes and organized my little stacks of paperwork, and I had to work with adults and some of them actually listened to me. This was a new thrill.

Although I had already worked as a babysitter and as a farm worker at Mrs. Bass's tomato farm, this was a real job where they paid me each week with a check and where people asked me questions and where I felt for the first time in my life like I might be successful.

Well, okay, talking about which can of tomato sauce to use for the cookout is not rocket science but I was passionate about everything I did. This was not just spaghetti sauce—it was Midnight Marinara. Snow on the Mountain was not an early storm. It was soda crackers, coconut, and chocolate. This job was a rare form of art and I threw myself into it like I was auditioning for a Broadway play.

It wasn't always easy but it was fun. I was outside most of the time, which is still important to me, and I was surrounded by strong, vibrant women who were trying to make a difference in the lives of young girls.

Mike probably never knew how much this job meant to me but maybe she did. Maybe she knew what it was like to never have a date in high school because you were taller than every boy on the face of the Earth and because your breasts looked like two withered peas and you could outwit every boy in sight. Maybe she knew what it felt like to have teachers pass you by because you had a big mouth and because when they weren't fair you stood up in class and told them about it. Maybe she knew what it was like to be turned down for all those opportunities because some other girl seemed more promising. Maybe she knew what it was like to feel that the entire world was waiting for you and that you could do and be anything if only someone, just one person, would give you a chance.

I bet she knew. Maybe she hired me because she knew and for no other reason. She probably didn't even care if I could make change and carry heavy boxes and cut open watermelon with my pocketknife and interact with a variety of personalities. She probably could have hired a ten-year-old to do my job but one day I think Mike watched me in one of the rare moments when I wasn't talking or acting like a jackass. She saw me writing a poem in my mind while I watched the rain hit the car window and then she saw me how I saw myself—brilliant, adventurous, tireless, talented, strong, vibrant, and scared as hell.

Sometimes, when she didn't think anyone was looking, I would see her sitting alone, looking out her tiny office window, fingers moving wildly, and I wondered what she was thinking about. Once in a while I could see a tense mound of sadness back behind her eyes that never quite eroded. She had a terrific laugh but Mike was as quiet as I was loud. She had a son who tangled himself in and out of her legs whenever he passed through the building we worked in and her husband looked like a movie star—tall, handsome, always leaning in to say something to her that no one else was supposed to hear.

That summer, without giving me one lecture, Mike gave me the world. She never corrected me or made fun of me and she managed to say something nice to me at least once a day. She trusted me and let my spirit roam in places that had been locked and bolted shut for the likes of the wild hussies like myself. She treated me like a person, like a young woman, like someone who is responsible. She asked me personal questions, imagine that, and I told her I was going to be a writer.

"Oh," she gushed, "that's perfect for you. I bet you are a wonderful writer."

Really? Really? Me? I couldn't even answer her because most people just told me to be quiet and probably wondered if I would even make it out of high school.

Just months before this conversation one of the cranky nuns at my high school had totally humiliated me in front of my English class. She made me stand in front of the class and read a short story I had written that I still think was just a little this side of brilliant. It was about a young boy who baited a deer all year and then during opening day of deer season could not bring himself to shoot the animal. The nun never talked about the story, which left the other students spellbound. She wanted to know why I had a run in my nylon that was as wide as the unloading dock behind the cafeteria.

I wanted to say, "Because I have a high crotch and they don't make nylons for tall girls and you have a stupid-ass rule that girls have to wear nylons." But I didn't. I just stood there with my beautiful words in my hand waiting for someone like Mike to come and rescue me.

Mike had some secret power that allowed her to see inside of me, right into my heart and soul, and she could look into all the dreams that I had stacked up—hundreds of them. She knew where I was going and she was opening the first door.

The last day of summer camp, when all the tents had been rolled into the back room and there wasn't a speck of dirt within miles, she asked me to come into her office. I saw her again after this only once during all the years that have followed but I remember what happened that afternoon as if it happened an hour ago.

Mike handed me a little box and told me she was glad every day that she had hired me. Oh! I wanted to cry and was overwhelmed by her gentle spirit, by what she had given me, by my own ability to stand there and not fall over sobbing into her arms.

"I had a lot of fun, Mike."

"People like you, you know that, don't you?"

"Not really."

"Oh, Kris, you are funny and you seem to get along with everyone. People are very attracted to you. Just be yourself. Always be yourself."

I didn't know what to say. She couldn't be lying. Mike was too perfect to lie.

"Open the box," she finally told me, smiling behind her crooked teeth, working her beautiful fingers along the sides of her desk.

It was a necklace. An agate from the fingers of Mother Earth wrapped around a gold chain.

"This is beautiful," I told her. "Mike, thanks for hiring me. This summer has been...."

Words seemed to disappear from my mouth. I was speechless. But Mike walked around the neatly stacked boxes and gave me a hug and told me that she would write me a letter of recommendation whenever I needed one.

"Never forget who you are and that you can do anything," she said as we walked outside. "Never forget."

I never did forget and I never forgot Mike. Thirty-two years have passed and I often open up my jewelry box, touch the agate stone and think about my real gift that summer. When my fingers dance on the brown stone I can smell ripe watermelon and hear Brownies laughing and I can see a young gangly ass girl edging toward the ledge of womanhood with a sense of power and direction that is worth everything, everything in the entire world.

Someday I am going to try to find Mike. I bet she still lives around here. She is smart enough to know that she may have changed my life but what she doesn't know is how I took her gift and passed it on.

She doesn't know about the little girl I hug in my own Girl Scout troop who has no one to love her and who tries to find me when I am out walking so she can feel warm arms around her shoulders. She doesn't know about the teenager I took into my home when her parents kicked her out or the other one who was addicted to drugs and just wanted someone to say, "Never forget." She doesn't know that I am raising my own daughter to think that she is invincible and that she can rock the universe with the edge of her hand.

She changed my world, that Mike, and there is no measuring that and my gift back to her is what I did with her wisdom, where I pointed my life, the hearts that I have held in my own hands because of what she gave to me that summer of the salt.

Soldier Boy

I am a ship passing through a storm of wars. It is the middle of the night in Dover, Delaware. One plane going. One plane coming. Boys, so young, lined up in their green clothes, eyes weary with worry. The smell of fear hangs in the air like a curtain that cannot be moved.

I am a reporter in transit from one war, while these men are going to another, and I am looking for any soldier from Wisconsin. Up and down the rows of men I walk, hawking my search like a reporter whore. "Anyone from Wisconsin?" I shout over the noise of sliding boots, bathroom doors, rustling transport papers.

They are all so damn polite calling me "Ma'am" and one rigid soldier points toward the back and says, "There's a Wisconsin guy back there I think."

The Wisconsin guy is tall. A young man, a boy really, in soldier's clothing. He is also beautiful. Young and tan and smelling vibrant, even steps away as I approach him. His eyes are blue and his hair, when it grows back, will be waves of blond. His eyes are gleaming with excitement and fear, and he cannot stand still. When he takes my hand, it is wet with a thick layer of sweat. It is that choking fear that comes out of our pores when we can barely walk, barely breathe, barely talk.

He's from a small town in northern Wisconsin. I can see his life as clearly as if I were his aunt, his older sister, the women who live one farm over. Everyone, this exact minute, is on his or her knees in his village. They are praying for this hero to come home. This football guru. This son and brother who joined the service to see the world and who is now hours away from a war that has already claimed the lives of many other young men.

"When did you know?" I ask him, while the world swirls around us, as we stand and whisper intimately, as if we have talked this way one hundred times before.

"Just a few days. We didn't have much time."

"How long have you been in the service?"

"Just six months. People think it was because I didn't know what to do. I've always wanted to do this. But now...."

His voice trails off and I step a little closer. Part of me wants to be his mother. Another part feels like his sister. Another wants to be the lover, saying good-bye at the gate.

"Are you scared?"

My hand is on his arm and we seem tied together. An awkward dance of familiarity erupts because we both come from the same sand. Our roots may have been crossed somewhere on the back roads of our lives all those miles away.

"You know they were killing them right when they got off the plane. Shot down a bunch of guys, really quick. I'm worried about just getting off the airplane."

When he moves to wipe his hand across his eyes I see a glittering, shiny, new gold wedding band on his fourth finger. Shit. He must have gotten married twenty minutes ago.

"When did you get married?"

"Yesterday."

"Yesterday."

Judas Priest. This is what war does to us. Decisions in an instant. Thoughts of never coming home. Insurance benefits for the girl you might have married anyway, probably, most likely, maybe.

"I love her. Really. It just, well, we were dating and we thought it would make sense to do it, just fast, before I left. Because, well, you never know."

Then she would be a widow. She would stand by the flag-draped coffin and tears the size of quarters would roll down her face and she would wonder forever what could have been, what might be, what should have happened.

I feel a slice of panic rise up inside of my throat that threatens to make me ill. My own then-husband is back there, miles from his wife, wondering where I am, how I am getting home, when I will be back where I belong.

My mind is shifting and moving so fast I feel like I'm on speed. I see this boy-man's whole life stretched out like markers on a game board. Back to college, a baby, working for that new company in Waupaca, a house at the edge of his dad's farm. Baseball in the old cornfield with the kids. He's a volunteer fireman and his wife ends up as a manager for the electric company.

Or not. He gets off the plane and one of those bearded monsters places a bullet just under the edge of his throat where I see his white skin smiling at me. When he falls, his rifle crashes to the ground and the soldier behind him trips, and when he falls on my friend, he listens to a breath that will be the last one. That gasp of air that seems like a beginning and an end. He will be back home in days. The widow will meet the plane and his mother will spend the rest of her life crying.

"Oh, Jesus," I finally tell him. "Look at you. Your whole life is hanging right here, isn't it?"

He smiles. He has not let go of my arm since we have started talking.

"Oh, yeah. Anything could happen. We're all scared shitless. Every one of us. The guy who says he isn't, he's lying."

"Your mother?"

"Cried like a baby. Me, too. I'm crying right now."

Wisconsin boys are like this. That's why I came back to marry one. They will stop and fix your tire. Lend you their last dime. Hold your hand even if they don't know who you are. Their mothers kicked ass and raised herds of men like this.

"I wish I could take you back with me. I'll be in Milwaukee by the time you get there."

"I guess it doesn't work that way. This is what I wanted, I just, well, I didn't think it would be so soon. It's so soon."

"Your wife?"

"She's like you. She's tough."

Men have been comparing me to their wives and lovers and girlfriends since fifth grade. Once an old boyfriend called me up the day after his wedding and said, "She's just like you." What the hell does that mean? Tough broads are not a dime a dozen. That is one thing I know for sure.

"You are both lucky. It seems like that."

"I'm luckier."

Wisconsin boys. Even when they are going off to war, you just can't beat 'em.

The line is moving and we only have a few more minutes. I want to press a button and transfer everything I know and feel into his arm so that he will be wiser than the rest, a survivor, someone who comes home to make his own babies.

"I have a son. He's just a baby really, but if he ever goes off to war, I'll kill him."

"I don't blame you."

"Don't be too much of a hero, okay?"

"I'll be careful."

When we get to the edge of the room, he stops and looks at me. There are tears welled up at the edges of his eyes and I can only think to kiss him. I grab his neck, as tight and tense as a clenched fist, and bring his head down to my level. Then I wrap my arms around his shoulders and I press my lips into his. It's just a Wisconsin kiss. There's a hint of his mother, his sister, and at one edge of my lip he can feel the throbbing heart of his new wife.

He grabs me when we are done kissing and he is smiling. "Thank you," he whispers.

He is gone. Just like that. Into the bowels of the dark night and I watch him hop into the back of the airplane and then he has vanished, into the black, into the war, into something that will change him forever.

When I get home I go to my son first. His hands are pulled up against his face. He is thinking, even in his sleep, and my tears fall into his dark hair and wash down the back of his head, dropping onto his pillow. I feel his entire body with my cold hands and I touch his arms, his legs, the hollow spot at the edge of his chin, his stomach muscles as hard as iron, his big ugly feet. Then I pull the blankets up to the tip of his chin, and wrap him up just like he likes it. "Cocoon me, Mom."

"Never go to war, Andrew," I tell him. "Be my soldier, only my soldier. Please, please, never go to war."

He listens. I know it. He is a Wisconsin boy and if he doesn't I'll kick his ass.

Becky Barton

The first time I see Becky Barton I know she is already dying of cancer. She is thirteen years old and has a set of legs that look like the sticks holding up the fence in my backyard. Her bald head is wrapped in a red bandanna. Her mother, Ann, is hovering above her—I think immediately—so Becky will not fall over and break in half.

Under my breath I say, "Oh, shit," and then move across the lawn smiling as much as possible, wondering how I am going to pull this off.

Becky likes me right away because I have learned to defuse every life situation with humor—even if it is inappropriate. I'm like a big sister, a camp counselor, the proverbial happy Girl Scout. We decide in minutes to be pals for life. Forever. How long can that be? Days? Weeks? A month?

Ann has the kind of skin that glows in the dark and a softness about her that makes me want to ask her to dance. I imagine she would lift me up and we would move across her living room floor like feathers blowing in the wind. When she speaks, she always touches my arm and her eyes, just like Becky's eyes, are blue and flash like blazing lights when she is speaking with emotion. Which she does every second of the day because she is trying to save her daughter's life.

Becky needs a bone marrow transplant. Becky needs money for the transplant. Becky needs me to help. Write a story for the newspaper I work for. Get involved. Never look back. Throw my heart into the air and watch it land in Becky's bony hands.

I quickly unwrap my hibernating energy and throw myself into this quest. I will write a story about a dying girl, her mother and father, and not having enough money or insurance to pay for the transplant.

That is what actually happens and my life quickly spins around Becky and her mother. From that first walk up the long sidewalk we become linked in the midst of a tragedy, a loss, a hopeful heartache.

Becky calls me and I walk with her around her yard—just tiny baby steps because moving can bring about a swell of physical pain. I make her a junior reporter and tell her to write down her thoughts, to let it out, to tell me how scared she is. Becky is like her mother. She is polite, generous, afraid to imagine the worst. But as the days pass and as she lets down her guard, she tells me things, and I feel her rocketing into my heart and I will do anything I can to keep her alive.

I am not married. I have no children. Just a dog. A few ridiculous relationships. There is no way for me to know about the bonds of mothers and daughters. No way for me to know what it is like to watch as your vibrant, promising, beautiful baby girl slips quietly into the hands of cruel, horrid fate.

Becky gets better and then she gets worse. The people who read my stories and the stories of others begin sending money for the transplant. Other parts of my life proceed ahead in orderly fashion, but most of me, my thoughts, my energy—it is all directed toward Becky.

The first time I fly to see her at the UCLA Medical Center the sky in normally stinky Los Angeles is blue and pure. I take it as a sign. Ann meets me in the hospital lobby with a smile that I have come to know as eternally hopeful and on that day, happy as well. Becky is doing better and she wants me to sit in on one of the transplant sessions.

My heart seizes up. Things like needles and blood and death and gore don't make me ill but I have this connection to Becky and her mother. I have already crossed the line from innocent observer to full-fledged accomplice. Inching my way up the long hospital hall, it is impossible for me to know what lies ahead.

The needle is the longest son of a bitch I have ever seen in my life. We are in an isolation unit with masks and gowns, and a view of the helicopter pad where the bones and brains of accident victims are continuously brought down to earth. The doctor is walking on his toes and moving so slowly I think he may be stoned. But, I find out fast enough, he is just as frightened as the rest of us.

Becky is glowing. Honest to God. It is as if she is giving off a small white steam. A mist of light. I want to reach my hand into it and feel the spray. Where this comes from I do not know. She has asked me to hold her hand and warns me that she may grab so hard, so fast, so tight, that she may hurt me.

Nothing can prepare me for this procedure. Becky's legs look just a pound lighter than the shins of a skinned giraffe. Her hip bones stick out at such a rough angle I think they may break if the sheet falls on top of them. Her head is bare again, she has no energy for scarves or hats, and her fingers, wrapped inside of mine, have only a hint of warmth, a hint of life.

When the needle goes in, I feel my lungs collapse, my ankles bend, my knees buckle. Becky is holding onto my hand and the side of the bed as the doctor lifts her with the needle. Her screams pierce me in a way that nothing has or ever will again. It feels as if I am swallowing little shards of broken glass. I try and move my head so my tears will not fall onto her neck. There is no word for this kind of pain, for this anguish, for bones snapping and blood as thick as sin, a life so young teetering on the edge of hell.

I may be screaming along with Becky. There is no way I will ever know but when I lift my head and see her mother I see a new world of pain. Pain so deep and harsh and cruel it is indescribable. It is a thick form of bleakness that I can feel like a coastal storm at full gale. Her face is pinched in a tortured grin, her hands are pulling against the sides of her own arms, her body trembling like an earthquake. Ann stands behind me so Becky will not see her and I am ashamed for all my trivial failings, for the fact that I am human and healthy, for every shadow that bends its way in between the passages of my own heart.

There is such relief when the procedure is over that everyone sighs and it is like a chorus of subsiding grief. The spent needle could cut a hole in the air, which is thick with emotions and longing, and a hint of hope that seems to filter down until Becky opens her gorgeous blue eyes.

"There," Ann says. "There."

I want to call my own mother and apologize for everything I ever did to break her heart. I want to thank her for cleaning my diapers and for wiping the vomit off my flannel nightgown. I want to tell her I am sorry for the one time I did not call her for all those weeks and weeks—and when she finally heard my voice, she broke out sobbing in relief. I will tell her how I was as ashamed as I have ever been in my life. I would give up anything, just that moment, to see her and tell her how much I love her.

Later that night Ann and I are eating dinner and trying to act as if nothing strange or terrible has happened. We are girlfriends now and this single act of horror, this cancer, will bind us together for the rest of our lives. When my own daughter is born, when I fall in and out of love, when the energy of my life splits and separates and I feel like I am sliding in between everything, when I look up and see that photo of Becky that has traveled with me for twenty years, I will think of her always, forever, now.

I snapped the precious photo the day after the transplant. Becky is a bald-headed scarecrow standing in front of her hospital room window. Her mother is next to her and Becky has her arm draped around her mother's shoulder, her Teddy Bear pushed against the small of her mother's back, her legs edged as close to Ann's as possible.

On the wall are dozens of Get Well cards and in the center of the bright window someone has pasted a smiling sun. And there is a bedpan, a package of needles, medicine bottles standing in rows like immobilized soldiers.

When I take the photo I have no idea it will forever hang on my wall and that every single damn time I look at it I will cry like a baby. I have no idea. None at all. I am as ignorant as the very disease that has tackled my friend Becky.

A week passes slowly for me when I get back home. Ann calls once and I slump through my days and nights like a zombie, hoping for the miracle, praying for the miracle, wishing for the miracle like I have never wished before.

When I hear Ann's voice again, I know. I know in an instant.

"Kris, she wants you to come," Ann sobs into the phone. "She doesn't have long. Maybe a day. She loves you. I know it would mean the world to her, to us, to have you be here, when…."

Oh shit. Shit. Shit. Shit. Damn. Hell. Shit! I leave on the next plane with a taste in my mouth as horrid and helpless as anything I have ever swallowed. I have seen death. Touched it. Waltzed through its early stages and marched alongside all its pain. But I have never been there, seen the mix of Earth and heaven, the light passing to dark, the aura of angels, the beams that pierce through a ceiling when a spirit is lifted toward heaven.

When I get there Ann and I hug in the lobby for such a long period of time I think that we will never be able to part. I need to be something for her that I have never been before and as we step down the dim halls and into the room something comes over me that I have never imagined. It is a power. A gift of knowledge, a sense of purpose, a spiritual calmness that commands my voice, my arms, every breath, the way that I stand.

Becky already lies as still as death. She is so white I think if she flipped over she would blend in with her hospital sheets. At the very end of her bed, her feet pop up against the thin blanket and I know that if she were awake she would tell us that the sheets on her bones are heavy, they hurt her. She is skin, bone, blood of the devil.

Ann's hands are all over her and she whispers in her ear and then stands aside moving her arm in an arch that lets me into this place, this private, mother-daughter space.

Becky's hand is surprisingly warm and her fingers slide into mine and I hold her there, next to me for one minute and then another.

"Becky, it's Kris. You can squeeze my hand if you want. I came to tell you it's okay to go. I'll be here. I think there are lots of people waiting to see you up there. You can take lots of notes for me."

There is just a slight pause. Not even five seconds pass and I feel movement in her hand. It is more than a twitch. It is good-bye.

Her breathing is so shallow I think she may only have a few minutes left. I pull my fingers across her face and brush my lips across hers and then I pull Ann back into this circle and step back.

Something holds me there. I should leave. This is more than a sacred moment but I stand there as if my legs are tied into the cold, yellow tiles.

Ann whispers. She is saying "I love you" over and over and over and touching Becky on her legs, her face, up and down her long arms.

I see it coming, and I am astonished and anguished like I have never been before. It is Becky Barton's last breath and I swear to God that a light enters the room. Becky's face becomes a sweet vision and all the muscles, all the pain, everything bad and horrible seems to leave her until she looks like a feather—light, soft, a glimpse of something that can only be thought of as heavenly.

I touch Ann on the shoulder and then I move sliding, sliding, sliding, to the door. I close it quietly and look through the window. Ann has wrapped her baby in a beautiful quilt and she is holding her in her arms. She is rocking her toward heaven and I hear the sobs even now.

When I run down the hall I tell the nurse that Becky has died. "Give them time," I say, barely able to speak. I find a room that is empty and I drop to the floor in the dark and I cry like I have never cried before in my life. I fall over onto the tiles until I am nothing but a ball that bounces up and down with each wave of tears.

In those minutes, I imagine Becky floating away. Her hair has come back, and she streams through this universe and into the next in perfect form. She feels no pain. There are no needles. The cancer is finally gone.

Later, I have to compose myself to call a story into the newspaper. I am so glad that Mary answers the phone. She is patient as I break down before and after each sentence. She asks me if I am okay. She can come write my death story when it is time. Mary is just what I need.

Years and years later, I am sitting in Ann's living room when I notice the painting of Becky that rests above the fireplace. A cry rises from someplace inside of me that I can't control. It is the same sound I made that day the doctor stuck the needle into Becky's leg and lifted her off her hospital bed.

In the painting Becky is almost thirteen and she has yet to be diagnosed with cancer. Her blonde hair hangs in waves to her shoulders, her eyes are a sweet blue, the color of the stones in my old marbles, and her smile grabs me by the throat. This is also a picture of my own blonde-haired daughter, Rachel. I am astounded. Shocked. Becky and my daughter could be twins, sisters, cousins.

Ann finds me in there by the fireplace and she knows.

"My God, Ann," is all I have to say. Ann smiles just like Becky smiled.

"Isn't it something? Didn't you know?"

"I had that one photograph before all the chemo but my wallet was stolen. I haven't seen this picture, since, well, way before Rachel was born."

"Do you think it's just a coincidence?"

Ann is a Mormon and she believes things that I cannot imagine. But I imagine this. I imagine Becky reaching in my womb and touching the soul of my daughter. I imagine her placing a notepad into Rachel's hands and whispering in her ear. I imagine Becky touching Rachel's scalp and tinting her hair just that way. Her legs, those fingers, a smile that can turn a head.

"Rachel is Becky."

I don't want to remember any of the horrible stuff but I can't help it. Ann has her arm around my shoulders and in a flash I see her holding that quilt and there is no way to stop my remembering.

"Ann, I never knew. Until I had my daughter, I never knew anything."

Rachel will be thirteen in just two years and then I will know everything. I will be almost as wise as Ann, almost as clever as Becky, always lucky to have known both of them. In my heart there is a well-worn path that winds its way in and out of all those days and nights and months—my Becky Barton year.

It is a path I keep raked and free of debris. I never want to forget. And on those nights when I hold my own baby daughter with her legs like sticks and her elbows jutting out like jagged knives, I sometimes whisper, "Becky, Becky" and listen for the echo that is reverberating through my own daughter's heart.

On My Knees

You can change the world by saying a prayer some people believe and I am on my way to the Catholic Church to stop the war in Iraq.

On this journey I bring both of my children who are toddlers. I also bring along a bag of food, books, toys, and a pleading, which is one step below a prayer, that war will not erupt in the pew while I get to work. There are only so many miracles. That is what I am about to find out.

I am so certain that my prayers will be answered this time that I have dressed and fed the kids breakfast hours ahead of schedule. I have not bothered to pick up the kitchen or flushed the toilets or returned any phone calls. I know I can do this. There is no question in my mind.

For weeks I have been staring at the television set while bombs blast and while we talk about war. Should we—shouldn't we. I am terrified, mystified, jealous as hell. If I had kept my journalism job, it would be my turn to go to this war. My turn to don the flak jackets and crawl on my belly to get to the only working telephone.

But my war zone these past few years has been my constant struggle between the alleged joys of stay-at-home motherhood and the once-felt passion, thrills, and idiotic love for my full-time newspaper job. I am always on the edge. Always.

Today I am strictly Mother. Goddess of Prayer. I am off to save my children, other mother's children, every child from the horrid clutches of another, goddamn, unnecessary war. I'm not sure this is going to work but I don't know what else to do.

The kids push through the heavy, oak doors of the church and run right up to the candles at the side altar. I let them each light one so they will not be thinking about it while I stop the war. In a matter of minutes, really, the President will decide if he is going to bomb the hell out of that idiot with the dark moustache. I had better hurry.

We sit toward the front of the church and as I place the books, the toys, the food on the pews, I notice that the church is littered with women. There are no men. None at all. I am on to something. I know it for sure.

I am by far the youngest female in the group. These are all grandmas and mothers and great-grandmothers. I am a mother-virgin amongst them and I bow to their experience. Who are they praying for? A grandson? For the boys from their son's football team? An old friend's great-grandson who is in the army?

Their energy is like a quiet rumble. It's a constant flow of power that seems to wrap itself around me like a well-worn quilt. Some of the women work their rosary beads. Two toward the middle have their heads bowed so low I wonder if they will ever get up. One in the front is sitting with her eyes fixed on the altar. They are sprinkled in the pews like little flowers that have been dropped from the ceiling. One here. One there. No one is in a straight line but these women form a mighty circle.

I don't feel quite so powerful in their midst. I am a novice knee banger but I am determined that my own two children should never go off to war, see a war, be worried about a war, or fear it happening in their own backyard. This prayer morning is unlike me but I feel so helpless—I have to try it.

I have already seen horrible, terrible things. Murdered babies. Women with their faces smashed in half. A young man with the side of his face blown off. Another beautiful boy with a drug-flooded mind and the body of a god. A blonde teenager, minutes away from death, searching desperately for one last glimpse of her mother. Bent women praying over their dead babies. A father gunning for the man who killed his daughter.

We have enough trouble without the war. I am talking with God now or whomever. I start out pleading because it is polite. My prayers are conversations and as I talk, I occasionally slide my eyes sideways to see how many Cheerios we have left. When Ms. Perfect, the daughter, catches my eye, she nods her head and folds her hands. She's a little shit who is hoping for a Happy Meal when this ordeal is over.

I go quickly from pleading to prayer, which is really a one-sided debate.

"It's so senseless, you know this, I know you know this. It never solves anything and people are still pissed off and hate each other and think of all those people who will die … for what?"

I am thinking this would be a good time for God, if he or she actually does exist, to reappear on Earth, maybe taking the form of a soft-spoken giant. I can see him, a shimmering figure in the hot sands, rising above one dune and then the next with his hands on his hips, legs spread apart, eyes wild with disappointment.

"What's going on?" he would yell. "I thought I told the world that we've had enough of this junk. Doesn't anybody listen? Hasn't anyone read a history book? Did Adam throw out a mutant gene that made half the world crazy?"

His mere presence would make people stutter and stop. Then God would stroll over to a tank and sit on it. Smash it into the ground so it disappeared. There would only be a tiny mark in the sand.

That would pretty much do it. Some wise man would dig a trench and everyone would drop their weapons into it. Then they would all go home, bake some chicken, and watch the evening news. "Peace on Earth" would be the lead story.

I've suddenly flipped from praying to dreaming, but really, they are one and the same. I let my mind go then and what I see startles me. It is first Andrew, my son, and then Rachel in military uniforms. This is the truth in my heart. This is why I have come to church. I am selfish. It is for my own children. To keep them this way, soft as the spring rain, tender hearts, smiling eyes, joyful minds—to keep them like this forever and ever.

Back to pleading.

"Oh, God, please stop this madness. Let it not happen so that there are no weeping mothers, no fathers with broken spirits, no boys with missing limbs. We can't seem to do it alone. We need your help. Help us God, please, please help us all."

I begin to cry. One of those almost-practiced cries so the kids don't see me and ask what is wrong. Oh, they know about the war because we talk about it but I am not ready to explain the nuances of my behavior, not just yet, please, God, not just yet.

Rachel has angled her way toward my knees. She is the busy one. Sitting still is not in her makeup. She can barely make it through *Sesame Street*. This girl needs action. Oh, hell. I am suddenly seized by the thought that she may want to do something like become a military jet pilot. Maybe she'll disarm nuclear submarines. Maybe she'll want to become a Navy Seal.

Now my prayers are furious. I am giving up on the war and asking for personal strength. Strength to accept whatever it is that happens. This day, tomorrow, for the rest of my life.

How will I stand it if she wants this? She already has the heart of a warrior. There is no stopping this, no stopping any of it.

I'll pretty much take whatever God can give me. That's what I have to go for. If the war comes, I'll have to dig around it. If Rachel runs off to military school, I'll have to bake her cookies and iron her green T-shirts.

I see this long, winding road ahead of me and there is no way to see what is around any corner. No way to stop the cars and trucks that slip over the line. No way to take a shortcut through the jungle.

There's no time left now. Just a few seconds to search through the crowd and wonder who will lose when this war happens. That woman in the back pew, maybe her old neighbor will call with the news. Maybe it will be the woman with the black coat who has not moved in fifteen minutes. It will be a massive heartbreak. It always is.

While I am gathering up all the stuff in the pew, Rachel takes my hand and holds it between her tiny fingers. Oh, sweet Jesus I have never seen anything as beautiful as a baby's hands. Her thumbs look like little cups of pudding and her fingers, already long and slender like mine, play back and forth on my knuckles because she cannot even stand still to be tender.

"Mom, is the war over now? Did we stop the war?"

My heart is breaking. I can't stop the tears this time. There is no sense to that. Rachel needs to know what she does to me, what the war does to me, how from this moment on we will be racing toward a sunset that is a color we have never seen before.

"I don't think so honey, but we tried, didn't we?"

"Are you sad, Mommy?"

She is trying to whisper but everyone can hear her. The women raise their eyes and I feel the hugs of a dozen sets of arms. I know that if I went up to any of these women they would hold me in their brittle arms until I ran out of tears. Then they would pray a rosary for me, fix lunch, and place a handmade quilt over my shoulders as I sat and rocked and looked out the window.

"Oh, honey girl, I am so sad because, well, war is horrible and some people will get killed and that always makes me sad."

"Oh."

She is thinking but she's also hungry. In just a few years we will be eating spaghetti at 6:23 p.m. and discussing the pros and cons of abortion. She will be swiping my lipstick and pinning up my hair before we go to the school band concert. She will be my daughter and my friend, and then I will tell her about this day and how the touch of her fingers, the sweet smell of her baby skin, the crumbs on her lips—how all those things were the answer to my prayer.

The Lump at 1:14 A.M.

It is 1:14 a.m. when I find the lump in my breast. It is a tiny knot of flesh standing guard just a little south of my left nipple.

It's one of those nights when my mind will not come to a halt. I am thinking about all the damn bills and work projects, and wondering how I am going to make it to piano lessons, tennis, and the conference at the same time. My back hurts. I'm worried about my parents and wondering if all these years of slaving over my words will ever make me rich and famous. I am always one baby step away from getting a new waitressing job.

My hands slide first over my right breast, which has always been so much smaller than my left breast. It takes just a minute to work my hand up one side, down the next, and toward the middle.

My left breast is a different story. This breast makes me look a little lopsided, not that anyone cares, and I'm thinking I must have screwed up when I nursed the kids. I must have skipped my right breast for more than a dozen feedings or something. My hands work this breast a little slower because I'm finally getting sleepy.

I pass the lump the first time as I check under my armpit. I feel it but I will not let my brain register this ugly fact. My friend, Joanne, has warned me about lumps in just this spot. She found a little knob under her armpit and then another. I find something there, it's just a little ball of flesh and I will never be able to feel it again.

But in my mind I know there is something under that goddamn nipple. It's a knot that I have never felt before. There it is and it hurts to touch it. Shit. I inch toward the side of the bed so I can look out the crack in the window. I want some air on my face. I want to scream and run naked down the street. It is a good hour before I talk myself into falling asleep.

The next morning when my then-husband groans, lifts off the covers, and shuffles to the bathroom, I roll back on my side and feel for the lump again. Oh, Christ. It's still there, and as educated and as wise as I am, I choose to ignore it.

I don't tell my then-husband about this for days and I never allow my fingers to drift toward my left breast again. But I think about it all the time.

This secret burns a tiny hole into the palm of my hand. I have already convinced myself that it's nothing but I check the schedule and see that it is time for my annual exam anyway. Of course they are booked for the next seventy-eight years. They can probably see me just before my Social Security kicks in. Then I say it. Finally. It is like the opening of a festering wound. A stretch after a run. That second after great sex. "I think I have a little lump."

They get me in immediately. Dr. Jill works her hands over my breast and finds the wide knot in just the same place. The little sucker has not moved in two weeks and I am off to the hospital for a megamammogram before she closes the door. I like Dr. Jill. We talk about men and books and kids and progesterone and women's health rights and all the places we could run off to if we just walked out of the room that instant. She doesn't think the lump is anything but she also doesn't think we should mess around. My mother is riddled with lumps and cysts, and this could be the start for me.

I watch her face as she examines me. She doesn't know I am looking but I watch. I always watch. She stops when she gets to the lump and massages it very carefully. Jill is tiny, about half of me, and her fingers are perfect for this job. They move like little dancers and again and again she makes me jump a little because when she hits the middle of my breast it hurts. She looks through the wall and I imagine her paging through a textbook back in medical school and wondering what a moment like this would be like.

Jill is cool. I think she might know it's nothing but maybe not really. I tell her to stop wearing nylons to work and to get some clothes made of cotton. She ushers me out the door and points toward the hospital. She is smiling but not too much.

There are two women waiting with me in the exam room. They are both pushing seventy and they look frightened. Our gowns are hanging open and little specks of flesh are exposed here and there but we don't care. We're girls.

When they leave, and I am alone, the technician confesses that those women have not had a breast exam in years.

"You're kidding?"

"No. We've been so busy it isn't funny."

"Isn't that good?"

"My feet hurt but, yeah, it's really good."

"Women have done a lot of work to let other women know about early detection. It's working."

"We're saving lives. That's what we are doing."

What is it? The statistics. One out of three or four? One of us will have breast cancer. It could be me. Maybe not today but maybe in two years or next month. Or it could be the woman with the hair as silver as my rings. It could be her and she will call her daughter and they will cry and then the daughter will be next. Shit. It's one of us for sure.

I have never had so many breast X-rays in my life. I love this woman running the machine. She is so gentle and kind with my little breast, which barely fits on the damn machine. She holds this mass of rumpled tissue like it's a piece of antique china, placing it on the machine just so and pushing me softly, gently, an inch closer. She has breasts. She knows.

When she is done, I am sent to the sonogram room. This is a new one. The last time this happened I saw my unborn baby's heartbeat. The woman in this room runs the device up and down a zillion times and whispers to me over and over, "Looks good. Looks good." She's not supposed to say anything but she does and she touches me on the arm, and I think that her warm fingers are the most wonderful things I have ever felt in my life. I want to kiss her I am so grateful.

Something funny happens then and they usher me back into the mammogram room. The technician is someone new and I am trying not to piss in my pants.

"The doctor wants a few more."

"Did you find something?"

"I'm not sure."

She's lying. I wish I was back in my bed and that I had never found the goddamn lump. I have this creeping feeling, like those ladybugs crawling inside your bra in late fall, that has moved from the back of my throat into my mouth. I can barely swallow.

This is just a little wait. Some people wait and wait, and then they go home and wait some more.

The doctor is young and funky, and she is a woman, which makes the whole thing a bit easier. She also has breasts. I bet she'd go out for a beer with me and tell dirty jokes. I like her immediately.

"The lump doesn't look like anything serious," she tells me running her long fingers on the X-rays in the dark room. "I think it's just a bit of tissue and I think it will go away."

I feel something warm spreading through my stomach and into the tops of my knees. It is moving like a shot of good Scotch. I can feel it heat up every inch of my skin.

"But...."

"But," I say sort of loudly. "There's a but here?"

"Well, I found a spot that seems to be growing."

"Show me, please."

There is something more than revealing about seeing your breast up on the wall like this. It's past intimate. Past anything quaint and quiet. It's like a special sacrament. The Medical Sacrament of Holy Breast Exams. I feel like I'm in church. We are whispering. The doctor's hand rises up to a dark spot and when she touches the glass the spot disappears for just a second.

I see it. She shows me my last mammogram and I see the difference. It's the same breast where the lump has taken up residence. That damn naughty breast. This mammogram shows it much larger than it was a year ago.

"What is it?"

"It could be just a mass of tissue or something else."

"Something else?"

"I can't say. We need to watch it."

She asks me if it ever hurts. Did my mother ever have cancer? Is there ever a discharge from my nipples? Questions that will help her figure out the end to the puzzle.

"I think it's best if you come back in a couple of months so we can see if this spot grows again and then we will go from there."

The doctor has moved closer and although I know it's not professional for her to touch me, I touch her, just on her elbow.

"You know, this is wonderful that you tell us right away. It's also wonderful that you are a woman and I think you care a great deal about what you do."

The doctor looks slightly astonished but she puts her hands on her hips and smiles.

"I love what I do. Women need to know right away. They need someone who cares."

Years ago I had a succession of positive pap smears. The doctor was a man and he talked about the lining of my uterus like he was talking about the grease under the bearings in his car. He said the word "precancerous" like he was jawing about his stock prices. He never touched me with a hint of kindness. After the surgery I asked him if I would ever be able to have children.

"Maybe. Maybe not." That was all he said. What the hell, I thought. You bastard. Then I drove to a phone booth and called a friend as I felt a wave of cramps breach my belly and buckle me in half. It was cold outside, and I pushed my head against the glass windows and sobbed for ten minutes while the greasy phone dangled in my hand.

"Can you help me?" I finally begged my friend while truck drivers barreled past and station wagons belched out clouds of smog food. "I feel like shit."

I don't feel like shit when I leave the hospital this time. When I get into the car, I pat my left breast with the palm of my hand and tell the damn thing to behave. I am no longer afraid. I vow to examine my breasts more than once a week. I'll start asking all my friends if they do a regular exam. I'll never stare out of the bedroom window again and I'll tell the important people in my life right away. I'll look this person right in the eye and tell them about fresh lumpage no matter what time of the night I discover it.

My next mammogram is on Monday morning. I'm going to take a box of donuts or a coffee cake or some damn thing with me to the breast queens at the hospital.

Then, good or bad news, I'm going to come home and do whatever I have to do. Whatever comes next, I'll take it and swallow it and make it a part of me. After that I'm going to have a glass of wine, even if it isn't noon, and I'm going to take my children, Rachel and Andrew, for a hike in our special place where the creek touches the big tree and where we have cast little molds of hearts in the sand.

When it's time for the next full moon, Rachel will come with me into the backyard. We'll stand under the clump of oaks and when the clouds pass we'll lift up our shirts and expose our little titties to the Mother Moon, and those rays of feminine power will keep us safe and strong, and us gals, we'll always be tough and strong and ready for the next lump. Always ready for the next lump.

Trick or Treat

The airplane circled and circled while I was out walking my dog. I heard it choke a few times and by the fourth pass I began searching for its shadow at the edge of the cliffs on the mountains.

The valley here fans out from one range of mountains, across a broad valley and into the gigantic arms of the Wasatch Range. There is a small city airport just on the other side of the lake and my eyes are scanning for something, I don't know what, but I have this feeling in the pit of my stomach and I am searching the sky for that little plane.

I missed the sounds of the crash. A popping—metal pushing against its own weight, rocks tapping into the fuel line, bones jostling like sticks under a heavy tire, grinding metal.

It only took me fifteen minutes to gather up my writing gear. Boots. A camera in case the photographer was late. Pens. Sweater. I keep all of this within arm's reach every moment of my life. I am Kris Radish. I am a reporter.

The police dispatchers know everything but even the dispatcher didn't hear the crash. It's because of the cars and the freeway and the way the noise shoots out, one way, and then another, in the mountains. A simple yell at the right angle can obliterate something as massive as the sounds of an avalanche.

Behind the state hospital, the mountains are a tangle of rocks and ledges that have never felt the edge of a boot or shoe. Even the crazy hippie hikers like me don't bother with those canyons because they are filled with bombs of rocks that can cripple a body in seconds.

The plane crashed back there. It glided into the side of the hill like one of those cartoons where the plane flies and flies and rams into the mountain nose first and then slides, just a little bit, until it comes to rest in a cradle of rocks.

The cops have set up a command center just below the Utah State Hospital. This same hospital used to be called the Utah State Territorial Insane Asylum and its history is a maze of mental madness.

Men with syphilis were housed in that dorm just below the ridge. Their shaking bodies slammed into the rails and they all died, first one and then another, after their wives brought them fried chicken and apples on Sunday afternoons.

In the old administration building groups of men and women dressed in rags and were hosed down while they sat on concrete floors. They ate out of metal bowls that were set near the drains and many of them may never have slept in a bed their entire lives.

Little girls with epilepsy were tied to wooden chairs and babies with heads the size of watermelons were placed in cribs that grew as they did until the cribs were as big as regular beds.

In the upstairs room of one building I once discovered an antique wooden chair fitted with metal straps and ropes that were used to give shock treatments to mentally ill patients. The wooden arms have what look like fingernail marks raked across their tops and I can only think of the word torture when I see the odd machine.

Today it is October and close to Halloween. The children's unit here is famous in Utah for its incredibly frightening spook house. Can there be anything more realistic than having a bunch of crazy, institutionalized boys and girls scaring the living hell out of you? I think not.

It's cold near the trailer, and I huddle with a few other reporters and the police chief as we dance between the wisps of our own breath. It gets a little dark and then very dark. Just down the road, at the spook house, they have turned on the recorder and there are moaning sounds, the cackle of crazy laughter, people screaming as if they have been turned inside out.

"Wow," someone says. "It doesn't get any spookier than this. It's kinda creepy." We huddle just a bit closer.

The Police Chief smiles and passes out cups of coffee. We shuffle. I try to shrink inside of my down vest.

Up ahead, on the mountain, I can see the lights of the rescue team dancing against the rock ledges. It is impossible to get to the crash site from the top. The crew has to climb, in the dark, on those moving mounds of porous rock. I am shivering but it's not just from the cold.

There's a slim chance someone may have survived this mess. But not really. An investigator is trying to uncover the flight plan. Who is it? Who was flying? Do we know these people? In the dark there are more than a few questions.

Soon the rescue commander begins giving us updates on his walkie-talkie. This doesn't help. It is as dark as a black hole. There are screaming sounds. Carloads of families are streaming past the command site.

"We have the plane in sight."

"Copy."

"No movement. We don't see anything but we need to get closer."

"Copy. We'll stand by."

The cops are focused now on what will happen next. There are ambulances. More rescue teams. Emergency supplies and the sound of coyotes howling at the fright fest.

"Oh, Jesus. Jesus. I see a foot."

"Copy."

"It's a mess up here."

Now there are horrid sounds that must have been recorded by a junkie on drugs. Low whining cackles, screaming—like a jungle filled with wild monkeys. In my mind I see the foot. A pile of blood. Scraps of metal.

"Beer cans."

"Copy."

"There are beer cans all over the place."

"Copy."

"God. Here's something else."

"Copy."

"Man."

"Jack, Jack, any signs of life?"

"There's no one here. It's a mess. Just pieces of flesh and body parts. A mess."

The men who belong to the relief unit begin to slouch inside of their vests and the ropes that are wrapped like large bracelets around their shoulders. The reporters ease against the side of the van as we wait for the next round of screams and the discovery of some fingers and the sound of crunching boots on the hills a mile above our heads.

Some things you can never forget.

Two guys drinking beer and flying an airplane, and below them the crazy people dressing up like ax murderers and those little kids next door getting ready for trick or treat.

The world. A rush of madness and the sounds of the season bowling me over year after year when I see the flying witch and the goofy decorations and I hear the screams at midnight.

Bloody shoes and fingers pointing toward the clouds and a wailing siren and always there is the wife who didn't know and the story in the afternoon paper.

Trick or treat and there is always another damn story.

They're Just Kids for Hell's Sake

The glass is as thick as the rim of my coffee cup and on the other side, from here to there, sits the murderer at this prison.

I would like to meet with him in a back room and sit as close as possible so I can look through his dark pupils and into the center of his soul. He is just a boy, really, as he was when he pulled the trigger of the gun that ripped through the neck of the other boy, just as young, just as foolish, and now dead while this boy-man winks and waves to fellow inmates.

What I need to know is how you can kill someone and not feel sorry or cry or wish to God that it could have been you.

Interviewing is my forte, so I think. I can whittle away at the edges of people's brick walls, their narrow passageways, the hardness that often forms over the soft layers of life. Usually, I end up holding hands, running my fingers across someone's arm, hugging them when they break down, and then, finally, they throw the details out that wash over me like a fine ocean spray.

But I cannot touch this boy. His dark hair and swarthy arms will never meet mine. He will crank his head, show me his new tattoos, and tell me what he plans to do for the next twenty years, but I can never touch him.

He will tell me how pissed off he was when those guys came into his yard the night of the murder and how it really wasn't his fault because someone else should have taken the gun away from him. "But the movie?" I ask, wondering in the back of my way-too-worldly mind, "You just closed the door after you killed that boy and finished watching the movie."

Well, he wanted to see the end of it and his friends were down there by the television waiting for him and so he finished watching it while the boy he shot was bleeding to death and still alive on the car seat.

Researching so I can write a magazine story, I rented the movie this man was watching the night he killed someone. Then I took it into my own basement one evening. My kids were asleep, it was quiet everywhere, and suddenly I was back there that night, just down the street, watching from the shadows of the pine trees I have already scouted at the murder scene.

It is such a horrid, grotesque, violent movie that I find myself jumping off the chair, covering my face, and dreaming about severed heads before the movie is even half over. Then I see the scene. It must have been running right before my prison murderer got off the couch and grabbed his gun. The way he did it, holding the gun sideways just like in the movie, is less a revelation than the simple fact that these people are all sick as hell.

I am watching the movie this young murderer watched, and then duplicated—step by step, the night he shot and killed a young man named Luke.

My writer's mind is alive with details that make it seem as if I had been there. Luke, who is about to be shot in the neck, probably senses it's going to happen. His long, wiry body would turn away from the gun barrel but there is no place to go, even on a night as dark as bloody hell. When the murderer pulls the trigger, the nine-millimeter bullet flies through the soft skin of Luke's body like a guided missile. It slices through his lung, liver, and colon and exits just a breath away from the spot where the doctor cut off his umbilical cord.

It doesn't end here as Luke watches the world fly in circles and slips to the ground as if he is falling from an airplane and has minutes to glide to Earth. His legs crumple and he lands in a pile and already looks less than human. On the way down, the murderer lifts his gun and strikes Luke in the side of the head, hurrying what has started so long ago—perhaps when he was just a little boy watching violence from his own crib—it is impossible to count the days.

Luke is already holding his arms toward the angels of death as this flipping movie glides from murder to murder. When he dies just a few hours later, he is alone in a hospital room and all the years that had once stretched in front of him are whisked away like those white milkweed seeds that drift into the sky in fall.

The murderer thinks it is cool to talk to a writer. When I leave, a parade of nineteen other people will come in to see him before he is sentenced to spend the next thirty years, which is really more like ten, in a prison where men will touch his fine, dark skin and where he will learn things he never could have learned in his own backyard.

"It was an accident," he tells me over and over again, because I keep asking the same questions and won't believe him. "They should never have come to my house."

The gun. I keep asking him if he always runs up the basement steps with a gun. None of my questions will have any answers. So much of this discussion is an endless paradox that started with some man beating his wife and empty beer cans and dropping out of high school and watching movies where shooting a gun to kill is a casual occurrence. It's like buying a cheeseburger and smoking dope until your brains fry, and telling the world to fuck off when you would really, really love it if someone just touched you lightly on the top of your wrist and said one kind word to you.

Our conversation rolls and rocks until I push him to the days and nights he will be spending in the prison with all the big guys. He still manages to swagger when he talks about what he thinks will happen and I know what will really happen. I know he will finally weep when he is backed into the corner and he has no place to go and the guards have already made their final rounds. I know that he will cry like a baby for his mother when he has his first bowel movement while a crowd of hungry eyes watch. I know that he will glance at a calendar and one day realize that when he leaves there will be a long line of worry etched into his forehead that will make him look like an old man. I know that in not so many weeks he will find Jesus while he is taking a drink of tepid water and remembering how the Southern Comfort used to wash over him and make him feel as if his life, the world, the universe were his, just his alone.

Sometimes when I drive close to the murder scene, I blink and it brings me back to that very night when the neighbors called the police and the tires squealed and their world changed but never really changed at all.

Then, just miles away, because it is part of my highway route, I often drive close to Luke's grave. I think about his frail, still-growing body, split open like a science experiment and how his mother told me she would have said good-bye if she had only known.

Mostly, I think about the waste and about the killer's black eyes, which must have blended into the dark of the night and that blink, that quick blink, just before a finger moved on the trigger and the rocket of steel moved over the lip of the barrel and changed everything and nothing, nothing at all.

Paper Clips, Two-Sided Paper, My Penis Please

There is no quiet way to sneak into the funeral of a widely respected man without being noticed. It has taken forty-five minutes for me to get up the courage to get out of my damn car and it's impossible to walk into the chapel without everyone noticing me, without continuing a lie that has festered within me for years.

I sit alone in a back row and pick a spot that will allow me to look out the window. It is late fall and the mountains are blank, filled only with simple spots of gray and brown. At the edges of some of the higher ledges I see lines of snow that make me smile. It's the silver lining I have been looking for.

One other person at the funeral knows what happened to me, what the now-deceased man did. She dropped her head when I told her the story and we sat together then, in the silence of her big office. He was still alive and, while I told her what he had done, his head bobbed back and forth just outside the door because his desk was in front of her office.

"Mostly," I told her, "I'm just pissed that he held it over me and that I took it for so long, so damn long. That's not like me. I don't take shit from people, especially men, but this was, well, I trusted him, I thought he was a mentor, a friend."

DeAnn doesn't know what to say. Her heart is filled with her own secrets and with the burden of asinine rules and regulations that have blown into our worlds on the winds of a trumpet played by a guy named Moroni, a Mormon angel.

I was sexually harassed and assaulted by this man, an editor who was my boss, pretended to be my friend, and danced all over my self-esteem like a short savage.

Our choices for retribution are limited, but I tell her that just saying it, just sharing the secret, has lifted a small weight off the edges of my feminine soul.

"Did he hurt you?"

"Not physically. Look at him for God's sake. I'm bigger than he is. All those short guys like my legs. It must be a big mystery to them or something. Like what's at the top of my legs is different from what's at the top of a short woman's legs."

We are laughing but it's just the beginning of what I want to tell her. Later, when she died so young from a bad heart probably brought on by other stories like mine, I remembered every second of this day. The color of her eyes, the way she shifted to put her arm around my shoulder, how we conspired to help all the others. I remember how she tried to tell me something else, something personal, that I was unable to receive and how ashamed I was later when I realized my own limitations. The hauntings of my life's mistakes and shortcomings seem endless some days. There's a line of "what ifs" that salute me like weary soldiers when I resurrect these memories.

"When he kissed me, when he grabbed me, when he tried to throw me on the bed—that was nothing compared to what happened later and I wish, damn how I wish, I could explain why I let him do it."

"Did he ever come back to your house?"

"No, but he was so sexual every time we talked on the phone, every time I saw him at a meeting, every time he gave me an assignment."

"I'm sorry."

"What happened is so stupid. I felt like it was my fault, which is a big crock of shit. I've never flaunted my sexuality ... well, maybe just that one time a few years ago."

We laugh again and this medicine tastes like fine wine in my bitter mouth. When DeAnn laughs, she tilts her head back and it is as if she is gulping air. She has a great laugh that bounces off the walls in her off-white office, like a reverberating caress.

"Kris, you didn't do anything wrong. He was wrong. He's done it to others."

This fact really pisses me off, and it is hard not to rise off the seat and bash his face into his computer. It was probably worse for the others. As unballsy as I have been about this, well, my God, the other women are like virgin creatures who have no clue.

"Was it bad?"

"About like yours."

This man came to my home, where I had my office, under the guise of a business meeting and then proceeded to attack me. He had the paper clips and two-sided paper I needed but he also brought along his penis. It was terrifying and humiliating, and emboldened by the release of this secret I shared with DeAnn, I decided to keep talking.

I tell her about the other editor who threw me against the lobby wall and shoved his tongue down my throat. I was not thinking that day, I told her, as if I should be on guard every moment of my life. I say, "You know, will the copy boy try and rape me at the milk machine? Will the publisher ask me to slip off my blouse before he gives me a raise? Should I have to worry when I ride in the car with another reporter that he's going to grab my tits at the next stoplight?"

If DeAnn swore she would be saying, "Oh, Christ. Anything else, anyone else?" I don't tell her about the last one. I hate to get carried away.

We go around like this for about an hour. When we are done, we have concocted a plan that will bring a staff psychologist into the fold. A woman, I pray to God, who will have to meet with inappropriate male employees when women like us have felt their fingers on a breast, a thigh, at the small opening just below an unguarded waist. It doesn't seem like much, but in this place, it is the beginning of a new world. There will be sexual harassment workshops and women will not have to go seek out a bald patriarch posing as a counselor when they need to talk with someone.

"What do you think?" she asks me toward the end of our meeting. "Do you think this will help?"

"I'm still pissed but I'll have to deal with it myself. Somehow. Someday."

We should have closed the drapes so we could hug each other when we finished but it was important to watch him out there, worrying, while we had this conversation, the beginnings of our salvation. Today we would hug, but today it's too late. She is gone and so is he.

I bring my anger to the church on the day of his funeral. Inside of me there is this tiny ball of hate that I have been trying to pass out through my bowels for a good five years. I have not been able to forgive him. I have not wanted to forgive him.

Men in dark suits and hordes of women in nylons sit and sing and smile. They are so happy because he is now poised to enter some glorious kingdom that the likes of heathen-me will never glimpse. It seems impossible. It is impossible.

DeAnn is up there near the front of the church. She has her legs crossed and an invisible dagger of hate, I imagine, hidden inside of her nylon belt. Now, I can't really know what she must have been thinking, how hypocritical it must have been for her to organize all those stories about his life for the obituary, how she mentioned the touch of his editor's pen, the way he pushed all those young writers to be and do so much more.

When the songs have been tied down to the back of everyone's throat and it's time for the procession and handshaking and for good-byes, I slip out the side door and gasp for air like a drowning cat.

Back in the car, I feel safe and no better, no worse for what I have tried to do. The canyons wink at me as I drive home, slowly and seductively so that I am pulled off the freeway and take the back roads that ride me so close to the mountains I can reach out and touch the willows where the creeks rise up to bathe the rocks.

This is what I need. Just a breath of the world as it was meant to be. Alone. Me. Always alone. Driving someplace. Waiting for some kind of delicious miracle to point me in the proper direction.

But on this day, when the clouds continue to float across the tips of Timpanogos like caressing fingers, I think I have followed the proper path. I have not paid my respects but I have sure as hell paid my dues, and the burden on my heart, which in this case rests just above the top of my vagina, this burden shifts just a bit and I feel like a new woman.

Not yet woman enough to forgive because forgiveness be damned. Some things deserve no forgiveness. Some things we never forget. Some things are meant to never leave the little bag of lessons hard learned that we should never hide inside the metal edges of our safety deposit boxes.

Even now, when I press the tips of my own fingers so deep into my heart that I can feel each pulse, every beat of my breath, I cannot forgive him and this, this gives me a sense of power that has obliterated even that last touch—his hand on my throat and his breath, hot as tar against my neck, right here, where I feel my life running like a river to an endless sea.

Eudora Welty

Her fingers are as long and fragile as the delicate toes of the birds that sit at my feeders. Her arms are swaying—limbs of a flamingo, I think, and when she moves to the podium, her body floats sideways and I can think of nothing but the swans bobbing in the canyon pond and how their beauty startles me each and every time I see them gliding, just like her, as if they are propelled by a force way beyond anything I know.

It is winter, and I sit in the front row pressing my fingers against the nylons I detest and crossing my own long legs so that when she makes her first sound I will be ready for the magic, for the greatness, for the inspiration to not run screaming from the face of my own typewriter.

I take notes, feasting on every syllable, watching her hands move—the bold eagle—and wondering how I can contain my awe long enough to make a story out of this for the early deadline.

Eudora Welty. Eudora Welty. Eudora Welty.

Here is the woman I want to be. Writing as if her heart were on a ledge. Living from word to word and caring not for the rest of the world. Typing a story that swirls from a place so rich in life and love and learning that I am gaining weight just listening. Blazing a trail as a journalist who swallowed the world she viewed and coughed it up in black and white so the rest of us could see it, feel it, taste it. Dissecting relationships like a surgeon who cuts through that imperfect vein and then patches together the mystery of disease as if she were God herself.

My ears are straining all those years ago to capture every word. I am wishing to hell and back again that I used a tape recorder when I worked as a journalist so that I could watch and listen and write all at the same time. I glance up in little segments when my pen is not dancing and see her lips forming words and those fingers that typed first, *Death of a Traveling Salesman* and then everything else, every wonderful word that has passed through generations of readers.

Around me students at this university where she is speaking shuffle feet and shift dozens of times. Books drop and some fools are daft enough to leave to use the restroom. They have no idea that they are sitting in the shadow of greatness. Here is the word goddess and if she should so much as glance at them, their entire lives could be changed. Damned fools.

There is no way I can remember even one word of what she said in her speech. I could paw through one of the fifty or so boxes of my writing notes I have stacked up in case we ever need to start the house on fire but not one word remains inside of me. Yet, I remember how she looked and stood, and how I felt cold and then hot and then simply awed to be near her. What happened after the speech is a near miracle.

Marilyn Arnold is taking my arm before I have time to bring my lips together. She writes about the writer and is an expert on Eudora, and when I see her watching the great writer I have this feeling that she has memorized every line of every story Eudora Welty has ever written.

"Kris," she says gently, not unlike a doctor about to tell someone they do or don't have cancer, "Eudora said she would talk to you for a few minutes."

I have just won the lottery. I am going to be rich and famous. My children will win scholarships to universities in foreign countries. My car will never run out of gas. My skin will never age. There will always be beer in my fridge.

"What?" I stammer.

"I told her you would love to have a personal interview. She said that would be fine."

Oh my God.

I rise like a queen. My attendants will bring my bag. Freshen my lipstick. Make certain I do not drool when I try to speak in her presence. Slap me when I babble. Place me on a chair because I cannot walk by myself.

Of course I have absolutely nothing prepared. I have not read her autobiographical sketch. I don't have the little list of questions I often prepared when I was beginning this absurd career of mine as a journalist. I try not to panic as Marilyn guides me down a long hall and into the sacred chambers of the university that is reserved for only the likes of stars like Eudora Welty.

Marilyn is as excited as I am to be granting me this honor. She has spoken with Eudora, sat in her living room, run her own writing fingers across the top of the desk where all this magic was created and is known throughout the literary world as the Welty expert. Me? Well, I am a wannabe who pens stories so inane when my reporter's work is done that someone should burn me at the stake. Marilyn is wise enough to know that I am a bird with my own feathers and wise enough also to realize that in a different time and place our own friendship would have soared like flocks and flocks of freewheeling cormorants.

I know this now because I am about as old this very second as Marilyn was then, and I have turned my own secrets and desires inside out and I realize what a gift, what a glorious gift she was giving me.

When Marilyn pushes through the door to the secret chambers, I walk past her and toward a cluster of velvet chairs that even then seemed very silly. What? Not leather? No La-Z-Boy? No rolling, sectional couch where I could lie down, take notes, and then faint in gladness?

Eudora rises just an inch, Southern lady that she is, when I move my hand toward hers. Her fingers are just as I imagine. They are soft and slender, and there is a hint of coolness in them that makes them melt into my warm palm.

"Thank you for seeing me."

"Oh, that's fine. Now, sit down. Ask me something."

This I remember. Every word. Her eyes darting, the way her ankles crossed, and then how she moved her legs, a sign of relief I think, out toward the coffee table. We have just a few minutes and I feel time ticking like little bombs that may go off at any moment while I try to gather my thoughts.

"Your speech was wonderful."

"Thank you, dear."

My comments are inane and I break into some specifics. I ask her about writing and her visit and what she is working on. How does she view her life? Did she imagine one day that she would even be here, speaking to thousands with an adoring wimp inching toward her feet?

"I just wrote and I loved it, and it has been my life."

The questions come from some hidden well inside of me that has been trained by years of interviewing. I know what to say, what to ask again, how fast I should push her as I see Marilyn glancing at her watch. Planes to catch. Words to write. Phone calls to make.

"Ms. Welty, may I ask something personal, well, personal about me?"

"Yes, yes go ahead."

She already knows what I am going to ask. I am such an ass.

"I'm a writer, but what can I do, how can I be a real writer?"

Her smile is a light at the end of a thousand tunnels. It is a caress after a misunderstanding. As warm and inviting and as kind as anything I could ever hope to see.

"Oh, dear, you should just write, write from here, and you will be and find what you need." She has her hand over her heart. Then she is gone and I want to sweep off her seat to see if there is a piece of lint, a lost hair, maybe a scrap of paper.

Years later, when I am reading her book, *One Writer's Beginnings* and still strapped to my deadlines, I finally see what she was trying to tell me all those years ago. It is so simple, like the love of your life who has been kneeling at your feet for years without so much as a glance from your eyes.

"As you have seen," she wrote, "I am a writer who came of a sheltered life. A sheltered life can be a daring life as well. For all serious daring starts from within."

It is this simple thought that makes me reach behind my own eyes to rearrange how I look at myself. When I do this, I finally see things so clearly that I want to throw away my glasses. This thing, this vision that I have been searching for, has jarred my teeth loose and I cannot sleep or eat or drink because my search has taken me around the world and back again, inside of hearts and souls, and through years of insipid research and disguise.

So I write like I have never written before, and then I pause and look at the woman I can see in the reflection of my computer screen and I see that what I have been looking for is right here—the edge of my eye, fingertips, my heart beating toward the light, and I see Eudora Welty rising through the mist with that smile as bright as all the lights that have gone on in my life.

Canyon Walls

My heart is beating against the red rock canyon walls a million miles a minute and I am traveling backwards in time. My feet glide across rocks and move me, inch by inch, generation after generation into the womb of creation.

Escalante. Escalante. Escalante. My mind is transformed as one mile after another moves me deeper into this ancient Utah territory.

My soul has come to rest in this desert wilderness and when I leave, as I always must, I wrap it tenderly in sage leaves and place it under the edge of the creek. It waits for me, patiently, while I flail my way through all the other days and nights of my life.

Today it is my pal Dusty and our dogs that grind up the miles on this canyon hike with me. It is spring and we have made a near-fatal mistake. Lost in this labyrinth of twists and turns we have not watched the sky. We have pounded from corner to corner silently, each one of us lost in our thoughts, and both of us high on desert dust. We have looked sideways and to the north and south but we have not looked up.

We go deeper and deeper into this canyon because we have never seen it before and because something unseen commands us to keep moving. We have not spoken a word in hours, but we move as if on automatic pilot, never bothering to call the dogs or look up.

Here, my mind is molded into a stretch of brilliance. I have taken to the canyon country like a duck to water and when I am not here this is all I can think about. At night, when the stars wrap themselves around me, I write so much poetry that I often run out of paper. Sometimes I cry but cannot explain why this happens. In the mornings I strip off my few articles of clothing and bathe naked in waters that seem to ride through the center of everything that I am or hope to be.

This day, we are walking like madwomen because we have to leave by midafternoon. We have not listened to radios or each other. This is and always has been a silent retreat into places that are nobody's business.

This is a church, a sacrament, a cleansing of hearts, minds, souls, bodies. It is a wilderness retreat that is as addicting as the fine wine I drink in my tin cup while I wait and wait for the night sounds to begin.

We are a good three miles into nowhere. We are looking for something but neither of us knows what it is. Rocks. Sand. A river that leaps across itself when the canyon narrows. Birds scattering from behind the bush. A strand of Indian corn as old as the rock where it has come to rest. The air. An ancient smell that lingers against the tight corners and seems to be a thousand years old. Sagebrush that calls like a seductive lover. Could there be more? We push ahead.

Lost in the canyon. The sky must have darkened on the top of the mountain a good hour ago. We do not see this and the dogs, who probably sense it, have forgotten how to speak English. They cannot be bothered with us and we march ahead, tangled in lost causes, broken hearts, our feet pounding to the ancient tunes of the Anasazi music.

We have water. A knife. Jackets. Matches. But that will do nothing. Peril is a word that does not exist in this Shangri-La but that would change if we would only have glanced toward the sky. It would have taken but a second, a mere second.

Sometimes the canyon passageways are so narrow that we walk for minutes and minutes inside of dark tunnels. That is why we don't notice that the morning sky, a blaze of blue, has turned dark. It is raining on the damn mountains and we don't know it. Not yet. But in seconds. We'll know it then.

The dogs come running toward us as if they have seen a ghost and one of us, maybe me, says "Oh, shit." This is actually a sacred canyon prayer that is meant to save stupid women who hike up canyons without paying attention to the important details. This prayer has worked many times to save the lives of dozens of women who have traipsed up other canyons. Will it work today? Oh, shit. Oh, shit. Oh, shit.

The water begins to rise so fast that I am astounded. "Flash flood," Dusty finally yells, the first words following our prayer. She is the canyon survivalist. I am a seasoned forest walker who would climb a tree if only there was one within fifty miles.

"What?"

I scream, trying to hold back the days and nights of my measly life that are about to flash through my mind.

"We run," she screams. "Start running."

Oh shit.

Oh shit.

Oh shit.

My leather boots propel me like rockets but the water continues to pound, first against my ankles, and then against the lower part

111

of my leg. There is no time left now for prayers. The canyon walls are so steep that it is impossible to climb up. We will be lucky, I know that second, if we get out of this sucker alive.

We run as if our feet are on fire. We try and fly over boulders and across small ledges that are not so slowly turning into deep and dark pools. We cannot stop to turn around. There may be a wall of water pushing just around the next corner. My thoughts narrow to just one single thing. Staying alive. That is all I want to do. The rest of the world, everything, it is all a blank slate. Alive. To live. That is what I want. Nothing else ever again.

The dogs are ahead of us and I begin to feel panicky. The water has risen two feet. We round one corner and then the next but I know it is a long stretch until we get to the dirt road where the river flattens out and there is space for all this fucking water.

We are so close to being trapped I forget to breathe. Dusty stops at the next turn because the water is so high we will kill ourselves if we try and cross at the only place we can cross.

"What?" We are both yelling. A second is like thirty-five years of my life.

"The dogs." Dusty must have thought of this because I am simply trying not to piss in my pants—like that would matter. "We'll send the dogs across and if they start to swim we'll try another spot."

They start to swim immediately and we move back a few steps. Still swimming. Swimming again. Oh shit. This is the very spot I stepped across less than an hour ago and it was nothing. Just a few inches of water. This would have been a great place to look up.

Finally, they swim for just a few seconds and then they walk. "There," I scream, my voice a vibrant stream of fear that moves now, like the river. "Go, go." We are birds on the wing, flying across the stones and the water is beyond my waist as I use every inch of myself to stand upright in the waters that are moving close to the raging stage. Dusty is ahead of me, smaller and struggling to make it out the other side. She grabs rocks and pulls herself like a shipwrecked sailor creeping onto an island. This is a movie. A bad movie.

The dogs have moved ahead of us and the canyons crackle with lightning. There is more rain to come. Much more. We run and we fall, and there is blood on our knees and racing down our elbows and smeared across the tops of our hands but we don't stop and neither does the water.

I am thinking now that we are going to make it but that is just a wish because we have to cross the river again. This time we have to swim, which is nearly impossible, nearly, because it is our only choice. The dogs are wild. They are not used to screaming women and they are torn between running for their lives and staying by us as we flail through the water.

This time we link arms and hands because the water is now bigger than one woman. It is a torrent of strength that needs to be listened to, if only we can cross this last time.

In the water there is only the moment of putting one foot in front of the other and whispering maybe, maybe not, and praying that one of us will not slip. A slip would carry us both against rocks and we would be dragged under the reeds and maybe I would get my boot stuck under a rock and then drown right there.

It is an inch and then a foot and then we know we will make it—we hope. Then we run like hell. I cannot think now how I managed to keep running. Something kicked in that powered me faster than I have ever run in my life.

When we reached the white boulder on the left side of the river, just after the fork, we knew we were going to be safe but we did not stop running and neither did the dogs. We ran and ran until we saw a green garbage can and I would not quit until I had touched it and the river curved toward the huge opening just beyond us and past the road.

For hours the water poured through the canyons and it rose as high as I have ever seen it and I knew that we had been minutes away from a breath that would have been our last.

Before we drive home there is a sudden silence, a mighty calm, and there are wet socks and pants and boots that will have to be remolded to my sore feet, but there is much more than that.

I have been whipped by the magical forces of this ancient land and I have learned my lessons. Although I have always been a good caretaker, it is obvious I must do more. It is not enough to hike and breathe and meditate as if I were some manic thinker. It is not enough to burn sagebrush leaves as a burnt offering to the gods of wind. It is not enough to whisk my soul under a bush and to pray for constant paradise.

In my heart I build an altar to the goddess of power, water, and red rocks. I kneel before her and ask for forgiveness. I say that I am an inadequate fool who has not listened to the throbbing veins of this pounding land. I have merely inserted my own heart into a landscape that is unforgiving. I have taken and not given. I am ashamed.

Then I lay more than my soul under that bush. I lay my sorrows and joys and all the hopes that have yet to form themselves into thoughts. I pledge my fidelity to this land and to the protectors of the universe. I succumb, as I must, and there, on my knees and then lying face down in the desert sand, I bare myself from limb to limb until I can hear that pounding, those veins popping and the quiet rush of a river that has moved back into its own cradle.

Dancing with the FBI

Tonight I am posing as a woman. I resurrect nylons, think about perfume, find a dress that I have not worn in public for ten years, breathe in and out slowly, wonder if it would be odd to put my thirty-eight special inside my cute little purse, and then I am ready for this enchanted evening.

Mikey is waiting for me in that goofy red car that he likes so much he bought two of them in case one of them falls apart. Once I asked him, "Honey, are you afraid you won't be able to learn how to drive another car?" Mikey is funny about things like this. He stores grain under his bed and belongs to a church where women are considered inferior. "I just like it," he tells me.

This guy is my coconspirator and we get along just fine. We have in common few things. We breathe. We live in the same city. We work for the same newspaper and I consider him my friend. We both have a sick sense of humor and think we are the two brightest bulbs in the pack. Sometimes I can tell him things I cannot even dream of telling anyone else. Tonight, for example, I am about to tell him I am scared shitless.

"me, too," he confesses. Mikey is dressed up like himself. He's a nice Mormon man, who is my make-believe husband tonight, and I am a slave to his every thought, whim, wish, and command. He has on nice black slacks, a button-down shirt, and that look. "She's my woman," he says without speaking. And tonight I am.

Well, hell. It's impossible for me to get into this. I am a flaming free thrower who can barely keep from smacking Mikey upside of his head. He thinks this is funny because he knows me and dislikes many things about me. I am a liberal who loves to drink booze and tell people to go to hell. I am as misplaced in this region as a barfly at his sacrament meeting.

But here we are and tonight we are going undercover. Truth be told, I love Mikey. Not sleep with, lust after Mikey, but love him like a friend, like a sister, like I love my female friends, although it's also true that I love some of them in ways that would make Mikey turn pale. Tonight I especially love Mikey because he could save my ass if this little undercover gig goes ballistic.

What were we thinking? Crazy-ass fools. Of course I would do it all over again in a heartbeat but in saner moments, which are few and far between, I shudder to think of the possibilities. Death. Dismemberment. Sexual slavery. My God. The possibilities are more than endless.

We take separate cars lest either of us thinks this is a real date. What is with that? Mikey is searching so hard for the perfect woman that he can barely speak. Me? Well, talk about a tangle of social contradictions. First I eat grass on one side of the fence, hear a whinny and then take a chunk out of that grass on the other side. I am a hungry woman.

Tonight, we are playing make-believe, so anything goes. We are always honest and that is why, I think, we found each other so intellectually attractive.

"Mike, I'm kinda scared."

"me, too. Do you think we should forget about this?"

"Are you kidding?"

"Not really. These bastards are nuts."

I love it when he talks dirty, which he only does around me. What a charmer.

"My God, we've worked so hard on this story. We are close. Don't you think we need to do this?"

"Well, sure, but that doesn't mean we should."

We both know we can't stop ourselves. In some ways we are no different than the group of idiots we are about to spy upon. People will threaten our lives over this, we know that, but hell, we are young and foolish and hey, are we ever smart.

I am sitting in his car trying to get psyched up to act like a submissive wife. No matter how I think or what I try and tell myself, I want to smack something. How do women do this?

"Are you ready?"

"Like what does that mean?"

"It just means the meeting is going to start in ten minutes and we should get out of the car."

"Oh."

Here's the deal and it's a frightening deal to say the least. These are the stories our mothers and fathers have never heard. These are the stories we would share around a glass of Scotch well into our old age—if Mikey only drank something stronger than hot water.

We are reporters deep into a three-monthlong investigation that hovers around white supremacy groups, two terrible murders, and an entire family that has fallen at the same time and hit their heads. Tonight we are en route to a meeting where followers of this goofy family are supposed to plot their next move. A prison break? More murders? A bake sale? We have no clue. Really.

I start looking over my shoulder the minute we get out of the car. This is some inborn reporter's habit that must resurface on undercover assignments. It doesn't help that we have to climb up a flight of dingy stairs in a building that looks like it will blow over if the wind picks up.

I go first because that's what little women are supposed to do and Mikey is holding on to the edge of my elbow, which comforts me, but just a tiny bit.

This abandoned building has one or two offices still perking inside of it and this radical group of men, all men, has staked a claim on a couple of rooms toward the back of the building. We step over boards and into the arms of these comrades who must be onto us, that's all I can think, because I am about as scared as I have ever been in my whole frigging life.

I really do have a pistol. I have been carrying it around with me for months because some jackass has been stalking me. I affectionately call him The Catman because he is after my pussy. This terrible man has called and talked about my underwear and about the size of my little titties. He wants me. He follows me. I am certain that he masturbates when he sees my photo in the evening newspaper. Sometimes, after I have been out, he calls to remind me what I had for dinner. He is a son of a bitch.

Mikey knows this and I bet he is wondering if I have the pistol on me. I do not because I think that it is possible these men will frisk us, or something will happen and I will pull out the deadly weapon and kill someone because I am such a wild ass. So I don't have it and that is all I can think of as I slink beside Mikey and link arms like the nice couple that we really are.

We are ushered into a medium-sized room that is awash in testosterone. I am the only woman. There is one man in this group who knows who we are and I am counting on him like I have never counted on a man before in my life. He is our informant and he's about as scared as we are.

He is scared because he thinks these men may kill someone else. They have made two murderers their martyrs. These crazy men cannot believe that just because these murderers killed two people, one of them a tiny baby, they should be in prison where they may be put to death because this state has the death penalty. Gary Gilmore learned about this the hard way.

These are men who think that women should always stay home and bake bread. They want their women to pick up after them, have babies on the kitchen table, and then rotate the garden crops while they polish their handguns.

Honest to God. This is as true as the worry that has worked its way up through the bottoms of my feet and into my calves, past my knees, bypassing my female organs, and is resting squarely in the pit of my pumping stomach.

Mikey and I do not speak at all but we are holding hands and the sweat pouring out of our palms is enough to make this building float away.

We are standing in a circle because everything in this culture happens in a circle. Imagine what you will, I'm guessing that happens also, you can bank on it.

Their words flutter together like a flock of migrating geese. They are so radical, so perverse, I think that in a million years I could not be objective if I had to portray their singular point of view. They are also in favor of using violence to promote their ideals, which is enough to make me vomit.

They are against the government. All governments. They refuse to get drivers' licenses and they try to pay their bills with bushels of corn and wheat. When one of them has an open wound or cancer they utter some prayers, slap on some mud, and think they are cured.

Children who belong to them are lined up like soldiers and taught things that should be outlawed from this universe. They are especially brazen about their feelings for women and I imagine most of them love each other more than they could ever love the fine lines of a precious female.

It doesn't take us long to get the flavor of this. These guys are angry and they talk about what they can do to get their pals out of jail. They are mad at all the other people who helped put their friends behind bars and a line of sweat trickles down my spine because if they knew who I really was, if one of them recognized me from the photo in my column, they would quickly build a cross and hang me on it.

Without realizing we are doing it, Mikey and I begin edging, ever so slightly for the door. Our escape. The light at the bottom of the stairs. Sanity. Pure thought.

I have never felt so creepy, so aware that I am in the presence of evil, and I have been in some pretty scary places. Every moment causes me to twitch and I watch their arms and hands, lest one of them says, "We know who you are," and then lashes out with a leather whip.

Mikey and I both begin running at the same time. It is when we excuse ourselves and hit the stairs. I kind of want to stand there and hug him because I am happy to be alive but he races to his car, me to mine, and we are away like one of those mountain storms that arise at the drop of a hat and soak the stunned world below.

Driving home, my hands shake on the steering wheel and I am aching to get this all down in my notes before I pass out with a glass of gin. I am writing, still in my girlie clothes, when there is a knock on the door.

"Oh my God," I whisper to myself. "They followed me. I'm shit. I'm toast."

I say this, and then I creep to the door and see two men standing there in suits. I look out the side window and see the car. Well, shit, it's the cops.

"FBI," they say as they lodge themselves in the doorway.

"Hi, guys."

"We need to talk with you."

"Oh, hell, you know who I am."

I have to show them my identification anyway. Then we talk and talk, and I tell them what happened and they tell me how they had the building staked out and almost fainted when they saw us walk in and how could we do that and didn't we know the dangers and could we please, please, please tell them if we uncover anything that they might be able to use to save a life.

"Sure."

When they leave, I start on the gin. I finish writing my notes, and I think about how evil is hatched out in some dark corner and then it latches onto the bottom of shoes and is dragged around and around until it is spread in places that we never knew existed.

When I bring my hand to my nose I can smell the evil. It has stuck to my skin, my clothes, this ridiculous outfit, and no matter how many times I bathe or how much gin I drink, for the rest of my life I will also be able to remember this putrid, retching, horrible smell.

And that is a good thing because we shouldn't forget all about evil and hate. We should never forget.

Death Sentence

Outside of the prison it is such a normal day. I have driven past swing sets and corn waving to me in the late summer sun and couples embracing and mothers whistling good-bye while the lunch boxes fly and the kickstands flip up and the baby in the kitchen hollers for attention.

The road around Lake Winnebago that leads me to the gates of the Wisconsin women's prison is a ride that quickly marches from strikingly beautiful to just this side of morose. Bad women. Bad, bad women and I am going to see the mothers. Just the mothers who are behind the bars and thick walls.

Motherhood has slipped into my own life like a somber slap. My woman-of-the-world genes, still not fully diminished, made way for the hormones of heaven that have blessed me with a son and a daughter who were never expected, never hoped for, never prayed into a life that has the head of a wandering compass.

My love for my babies is as fierce as anything I have ever known or can ever hope to know again. I would claw my way up the side of a steel mountain for them. Flip over dump trucks. Beat the living hell out of anyone who looks at them sideways. Walk naked into the local grocery store. Tell my deepest, black-as-night secret.

They are the focus of my nights and days, and a moment without them is unthinkable.

That is what brought me to this huge sliding gate where I press my face against a window, show my identification, and slip past a fountain of barbed wire that looks like a meteor shower from hell.

I am writing about women in prison who are mothers. Mothers. Imagine. Concrete walls filled with pictures made with tiny fingerprints. Visits where mommy goes away in handcuffs. A sprinkling of phone messages that melt the phone in rivers of tears. Bad, bad women.

This is not my first visit to this prison. I have been here for other stories and to interview other mothers for this magazine piece. But today I am interviewing a woman who is about to die.

Lori Iglesias has the HIV virus and she will be dead in less than a year after I interview her. She knows this and I know it and so do her two boys who live back home in New York City with their grandma.

I have stuffed my bag with candy bars and my heart with good intentions because that is all I am allowed to give her. The prison bigwigs do not necessarily like me but they cannot keep me out. So they will watch me and someone will yell through the window when I hold Lori's hand and they will not let me hug her good-bye but I will find a way to do it anyway.

But first I have to walk down the long halls, listen to the cackles, and have several women call me beautiful, and I smile and wink at all of them. It's the least I can do. Just my small gift to the women's prison movement.

They put me in a room with a table so long I think they could do surgery on a giraffe on top of it. What could they possibly do in here? I just want to talk, but mostly listen—that's my specialty.

Lori and I have met over months of letter writing. She wants me to know who she was and most importantly who she is now. Seriously, Lori is a lightweight. I have already spent hours with two murderers and a woman cop who fell in love with a convict and slipped him a gun. Really, Lori, you are not so bad.

Prostitution. Just that one crime, but then she took one step further, pimping girls in a nice college town so she could take a day off now and then and rest her body. Lori, Lori, Lori, what were you thinking?

Not much apparently, and drinking and drugs and not about the babies who were here and there and then mostly gone until she was caught and then the HIV. Now I see her coming through the door and she looks like a walking dead woman. An explosion of pity washes up from inside of my stomach and I have to stifle a cry.

"There you are. Hi, Lori. Thanks for coming."

"I have to talk to someone," she says, sitting quickly, fidgeting, not able to look into my eyes.

Her eyes are as dark as the bleak metal door in this room and everything about her—her slouching shoulders, arms that can barely rise to the table, hair limply pulled behind her ears, reeks of tiredness and surrender.

"How do you feel?"

"Terrible, I need to get out of here. There isn't much time left. Maybe a few months. I need to see my boys."

I push her the candy under a pile of papers and she slips them into her pockets as if they are gold bars and I tell her I wish there was something else. "This is enough," she says and rewards me with a smile.

Our talk rambles from the crimes, to her upbringing, and back to her boys. She has watched them grow from babies into young adolescents inside this prison, and when she talks about them she acts as if she sees them, standing right here, and her hands move involuntarily as if she were pressing their arms or brushing the hair from their eyes.

She has only seen them a handful of times, and she has told them everything about her life and her mistakes and about feelings of loss that can never be repaid.

Lori is one of the women who has managed to learn something from prison. She has worked with young prisoners, counseled them, and been involved in an outreach program that has women prisoners talk openly about what really happens when you give up everything. She has talked about AIDS and she has spent every minute of every day hauling around a satchel of guilt that is immeasurable.

"There is no crime in the world worth this," she tells me. "I've given up years with my boys and I've lost moments that I will never get back."

These are the interviews they don't prepare you for in journalism school. They teach you how to use commas—which I totally ignore—and they tell you that you will never be rich, but they never teach you about holding hands and listening until the moment before you think your own heart will pop. There is nothing wrong, I have learned myself, in bringing along your own soul to a place of darkness.

Lori puts her head on the table and cries softly as she tells me what the boys are like this very day. She knows when they get up, what they watch on television, and how a girl in math class has a crush on her oldest son. She has never seen any of this but imagines it twenty-four hours a day, every day, every long night.

"The crimes," I ask her gently, because there is no getting around her choices. No getting around the need for punishment.

"You don't think about it at first. You do things that are wrong and you don't think. I was foolish and there was this man and now I pay for it all the time."

She wants to know about my babies, and I tell her as much as the time allows and I see her trying to sneak into my eyes so that when I leave she will go with me and then help me pick up the kids and make dinner and give them baths while I sing them those stupid-ass songs they love to hear.

It is painful for me to talk about them, with her, even though I know what she did was wrong. Even though being in prison has given her a few extra months of life. Even though I get this story. Maybe I feel guilty because I have never been caught. My crimes have mostly been of the heart, and although I have been punished, I think suddenly that I have gotten off easy.

"Lori, at night, what do you think about?"

The tears are running now into a lake that has formed on the edge of her prison shirt. I can see it spreading, fanning out like a huge wet dot on a paper towel, and she talks through this mess and tells me about warm feet against her legs and the sighs in the kitchen and walking to the playground. Simple things. Lost moments. Sorrow and anguish that fills up the room until I want to run to a window—if only there were such a thing.

I know that this will be the last time I will ever see Lori Iglesias alive. She is hoping for early release because there are so few days left. And Lori is released just a few months after the interview and ironically loses her eyesight not long after she gets home. But she sees long enough to memorize the lines in the faces of the boys and knows how they have come to lie on their stomachs when they watch television and how they eat with their elbows on the table.

She dies just a few weeks later and when I hear of this, I cry like a baby for reasons so numerous I don't even bother to count them.

I just cry and cry, and then I crawl into bed with my own babies and I strip off their clothes and hold them naked against my breasts so that when we breathe it is as if we are just one lump, one mass of mother and child.

And I think always, always, about how terrible it is to punish the babies as well as the mothers. I think of Jean Harris and the programs where women can have their babies and keep them, and I know the statistics about recidivism and I think shame, shame on us for punishing the babies who will grow up to be angry adults and this damn circle gets larger and larger and shame, shame on us.

The Night of the Jackass

Night on the Montana Hi-Line, a pathetic stretch of road that waves across the entire top of the state like a bad dream, is not unlike driving into the arms of hell. It is black and bleak, and the wind blows so long and hard that cars and wagons and trucks are sometimes flipped into the ditches like Tinker Toys.

Tonight I am logged to the gills with coffee and it's raining and blowing like a son of a bitch. My Toyota Land Cruiser, with the little radishes painted on the side, feels like a lost grenade, ricocheting from gravel to highway and back again.

I am a professional Girl Scout. Honest to God. My work carries me for hundreds of miles from one section of the state to the next where I train leaders, raise money, do publicity, and pretty much stand on my head if that's what someone wants me to do.

This is a perfect job for a twenty-one-year-old woman with a journalism degree and the guts of a rodeo queen. Nothing much scares me because I am young and stupid. Inside of the Toyota I carry a survival kit, a big hunting knife, sleeping bag, and a huge wool blanket to keep me warm while I drive. When it snows, my doors fly open and I get an actual snow drift in my passenger seat. It's better than groovy.

Three days on the road and I am brain dead, lonely, and in that state of mind that keeps me wondering what is happening in the real world. I have already spent twenty hours in a plastic restaurant booth because of a whiteout—snow so pure that it blots out the horizon, the road, the breath beaming from your own body. When I spy a line of red brake lights that reminds me of Christmas decorations, it is easy to be momentarily confused. There are never many cars on this lonely island of a highway. Something is going on. Probably the damn wind.

All the cars have stopped and I see a tall man moving from car to car, sticking his head in the windows, and then moving on. He looks like a Montana guy. Swarthy. Dark hair. Red wool jacket. Cowboy boots. Chew bulging from his back pocket.

"Hey."

"Hey."

"A truck slid over in the mud and the road is blocked. It could be a while."

"Man."

"Can you wait?"

"I live in Havre. I don't have anyplace else to go."

"me, too. Are you married?"

This is when I should have told him I was married to a professional female wrestler who ate men's legs for breakfast. But no, I tell him I am not married and I give him my phone number like a young fool. This will prove to be a strange and sad mistake.

He calls. I am thinking about the guy who owns the hardware store who barely comes up to my shoulder who has been following me around town like a sad puppy and I say yes, I'll go out with you. What could be worse? The bars in this town are filled with drunks who drool and think good sex means staying awake until your pants have slid past your knees. All the sane, single people have left years ago. I am definitely not myself here.

He picks me up in a cattle truck and we are going to a rodeo, which is kind of cool. He reeks of marijuana and hands me some. I am living in a town where the people I work with know what time I go to the bathroom. It is not a good idea, I tell him, for me to get stoned in public with a man I do not know.

"Okay," he says, then asks me to drive and hops in the passenger seat.

Cattle trucks are unwieldy beasts. The wire cage sticks out over the top of the truck and if I turn just a little it feels as if the truck is going to fall over. We are off to the rodeo. Yeehaw.

He starts drinking beer at the rodeo and I am getting panicky. I really can't call anyone because, well, I don't have any friends. Carolyn, my soul sister and a coworker, lives six hours away but that's asking a bit much. I watch the rodeo and pray to God that the hipper of booze in his back pocket is already half empty because he's also doing shots of rot-gut whiskey that smells like his first horse.

I start asking to go home about forty-five minutes into the date. Yes, I am a party girl but this large man is scaring the living hell out of me. He is loud and swaggering, and my mind is already filled with graphic pictures of the terrible things he could do to me before I poke his eye out with the pencil on the dashboard.

When we get close to my apartment he laughs and swings the truck away from my back-door driveway. That little woman who lives in my stomach and rises up to nip me in the throat in times of great stress makes a grand appearance. She is pushing adrenaline through my veins like a junkie. I am scared now and wondering how badly it would hurt to simply fall out of the truck and onto the concrete highway.

"I want to take you for a ride," he slurs.

"A ride?"

"Yep. Let's go out to the reservation and drive around."

Oh, great. This is the same reservation that I am not allowed to drive through for my work duties because there have been more than a few terrible things going on. A rape. Some shootings. Protests by the Indians who deserve to complain every day of their lives.

Before I can think about what to do, we are heading down the longest, blackest highway in the world. It is a tunnel of darkness, a bleak and barren jaunt into hell. Then he reaches over and pulls a gun out of the glove compartment.

"What is that for?" I boldly ask.

He turns and looks at me slowly with his glazed, dark eyes and I realize he is probably doing more than just pot and booze.

"You just never know what could happen out here."

I ask to go home again and inch as close to the door as possible. He doesn't say anything but he drives and drives deeper into the dark night. He keeps the gun by his right thigh, just close enough for him to grab it in a flash, you know, in case something happens.

I am suddenly sorry for every terrible thing I have done in my life. I promise to stop dating men. I will become a missionary in Africa. I will sell my few meager possessions and donate the money to the poor. I am convinced that I will never see my mother and father again.

We drive and drive and drive, and I try and stay alert so I can be ready for anything. I decide to just shut up because maybe he will forget I am there. Maybe he will just fall asleep, and I will throw him into the ditch and drive this damn truck off a cliff and then sleep under a bush until morning.

Hours pass, my life flashes in front of my eyes so many times I can see the freckles on my own back and I finally have to pee. He pulls over by some trees and as I am squatting out there I am tempted to walk into the darkest spot on the horizon and hope that he will leave. This is foolish, of course, because there are wild animals out here and it is cold outside and I sadly decide my chances are better with him. How pathetic.

He stops talking, finally, and I watch the stars and lines of trees, and I continue to make more promises than I will ever be able to remember.

He edges back toward town and I get a glimmer of hope. Maybe he won't rape me. Maybe he won't shoot me in the head. Maybe he won't tie me with that twine to the back gate and pull me down the highway. Maybe he won't push my head down between his legs with those hands as large as hubcaps. These are definitely happy thoughts.

At the edge of town, he teases me again and I sit rigid, like a broken doll with legs and arms that will not move. He gets close to my apartment and then drives away again. I act like I don't care but that damn gun is still sitting right there. A part of me wants to grab it and shoot him in the leg so he will be crippled for the rest of his life. That's the least I could do for him, that bastard.

When he rounds the corner, I am pissed. I have been practicing this in my mind and I reach over, unlock the door, place my hand hard against the back of the seat and I throw myself out of the truck. I land on my feet and start running for my front door, which is about a block away. I am lightning and wind and a wronged woman. My key is in my hand and I unlock the front door, run up the steps, and slam it behind me.

I don't look out of the window, but in one of those rare moments of superhuman strength I somehow push my huge metal desk, which is the size of a corn picker, all the way across the room so it is braced up against the door. Then I crawl on my hands and knees to the window to see if he is looking. I see his tail lights out there and wonder if he will try and come in. He's probably taking a piss in the gutter. I pray that someone will rear-end him and send him sailing through the stop sign like a ship in a hurricane.

I see the lights of the county jail across the street and it gives me some comic relief. Bad guys. Just over there. All locked up. Isn't that funny?

I sleep that night right on the floor behind the desk with a knife in my hand, fully clothed with my running shoes strapped to my feet. In the morning I don't actually wake up because I have never really been asleep.

What is it about the light? The comfort of morning, the sound of the women coming to work in the downstairs office, the smell of coffee wafting through the air on the wings of angels, voices in the alley, traffic picking up, and all the damn cowboys back on the ranch where they belong.

He never came back. I saw him once or twice around town, and I wonder if he even remembered that he had taken me to the rodeo and all those other places.

But I remembered and I took this giant step inside of myself to a place, which demands to this day, that I take a long, wide gander at any man approaching my life. I rode with other men eventually, glancing sideways, keeping my hand on the door, my heart locked forever in a secret compartment and I have always managed to avoid roadblocks on the nights when the wind picks up and there is a chance of a mudslide.

Aunt Barbara's Eyes

Once, when I was a little girl and spending my special summer week at her house, Aunt Barbara and I got all dressed up like we were going downtown to work. Uncle Ron, her husband, met us at this place called The Buttered Bun, and we sat on stools at the busy counter and ate hamburgers and Aunt Barbara told me about her life when she worked as a secretary.

I was spellbound. Little Krissy was just a little girl from the country who was in the big city with my patent leather shoes. I remember how the lady behind the counter smeared butter as thick as my arithmetic book on the buns, and then set them gently on the grill until they sizzled like burnt marshmallows.

Everyone wore suits and dresses that had those goofy waist belts and nylons and high heels with pointy toes that made me wonder how they could walk with their little toesies jammed in there.

Auntie Barbara talked to me during lunch and all of the time like I was her friend and not just her niece. When she walked she kept her arm bent and her purse angled just in front of the middle of her waist as she traveled down the sidewalk.

After lunch that day she took me to her old office and all the ladies came to see us, and they gave me candy that was in an old cigar box. I was the princess and Auntie Barbara was a queen, and I walked through the busy streets and made believe I was on my lunch break from the big office with the glass windows.

Later, in her tiny backyard that was so small they had a power mower with an electric cord on it, we laid out our towels on the lawn chairs and smothered ourselves in Coppertone. Then we fried in the sun and talked and held hands and drank lemonade until we had to run inside and go potty.

Ha! My brothers and sister were home in Big Bend playing on the back road and dragging frogs behind their bikes, and I was in the big city, and this was always the most glorious week of my life.

Aunt Barbara swore and talked out of the side of her mouth, and when she laughed it sounded like a train coming at you and there was absolutely no time to get off the tracks. People thought she was my mother with her long legs and blue eyes, and how she sauntered and looked as if she was always going to tell someone to go to hell. When she took me grocery shopping she always parked in the middle of two spaces and said, "They can kiss my ass." She was my hero.

So much later when she adopted those two babies and then she got pregnant and I watched her pounding that poor sick little girl with the diseased lungs who only lived for a few months, I always thought about the day we had those hamburgers. I could close my eyes and see the pickles lined up on the edge of the plate and smell the fried onions and taste that butter, like liquid gold, running down the back of my throat.

Then years and years of anguish fill up her own lungs and liver and stomach, and I am walking through the hospital doors to say good-bye to her because her stomach is as big as a stuffed pillow and they can't get all the cancer out. She is so goddamned young and she is my Auntie Barbara.

I am not so brave when I see her in the bed and everyone looks at me, gets scared, and decides to leave for a moment. I want to crawl into bed with her and tell her that I love her and that she has always been my favorite Auntie. I have told her this before, and she knows it, and I should be able to say it again but I can't because every single word that I know is buried under a bushel of tears.

The room is a whirl of tubes and basins and that smell, that damn smell of sweat and years of life and longing and sadness that passes through my heart and makes me see that it was so wise of me to come, this day, this very damn day because it is hours, mere hours till her eyes will fade and the room will grow dim.

I want to crawl into bed with her and wrap my own long legs around hers and ask her if she remembers all those afternoons when we smelled of Coppertone and then ate sandwiches for dinner and drank soda, which I was rarely allowed to have at home.

I want to tell her about the day my cousin Susie and I filled up her sink with too many suds and how we pushed them out of the kitchen screen and into the backyard. "It looked like snow," I would tell her.

I want to tell her I am sorry her son Tommy killed himself and left her with all those years of wondering. I want to tell her how proud I was every time someone thought she was my mother.

But I can barely touch the bed without her rolling her eyes in pain toward the ceiling.

"I shouldn't have let them cut me open this time, Kristy," she tells me, calling me a name only my father also uses.

"You had to try."

"Oh, honey. It's a pisser. A real pisser."

She is talking about the pain, and I wonder if any of these people standing guard knows to ask for the medicine and if they can push around any lazy nurses. But then I realize we all have the same blood and that no one or nothing pushes us around— except cancer and death.

The small talk is not easy. But I still don't know what to say, which is such an odd thing for the Queen of Mouth.

We only have a few minutes because no one wants to be away from her for very long. It is the damned death watch and her sister and my uncles and her husband and daughter are grinding themselves into the floor out in the hall.

I finally push my hands against the sides of her face and bring my head down to her lips. In the time it takes for me to move down there, two seconds, I fall into her blue eyes. Eyes the color of a summer sky and the identical baby-blue eyes of my father. Eyes that bug out like mine and then fly from side to side because we/she are always looking for something new, something funny, something to say. Inside of her eyes I am swimming in her same tears and I have my arms around her like we used to do on the couch when Aunt Barbara folded up like a little raccoon and we were warm and safe and happy—forever.

She brings up her hand to touch me on the arm. Her fingers are cold and white and as thin as the tubes that come out from under the sheets. They move just once, then twice on my warm skin and it is all she can do, this simple movement that will later bring me to my knees when I am in my own living room.

Auntie Barbara died the next day, and when I close my eyes now, I can walk inside of those baby blues and I can see her laughing at what some asshole just said on the radio and pulling up her swimming suit straps until they snap and eating all the potato chips that curled in half and playing with the ice cubes in the glass on the table and telling me in her throaty voice to never smoke those goddamn cigarettes but to always keep my breasts high, pointed right toward their eyes—"knockers up baby" and to never take shit from anyone.

It Used to Really Be Something

Judy told me right off the bat that this was the guy who got stuck on the toilet.

"It was for hours I think," she told me, raising her eyes that seemed to swirl in left-to-right circles under her blonde bangs. "It's a good thing we had someone coming."

"What happened?"

"Well, she just lifted him off because he's like skin and bones and then well...."

"Well, what?"

"Well...."

"Judy, I'm a big girl. Actually, some people think I'm close to large."

"He felt her breasts."

I started laughing because I can see this in my mind and I know the woman she is talking about who had her breasts felt up. She has a kind heart and willing arms, and she would have smiled about the whole thing.

"I love it."

"Well, just so you know, in case he doesn't answer when you stop, he may be stuck on the toilet."

Delivering Meals on Wheels is indeed a wild adventure. It is also a sad commentary about how many of our senior citizens are left to rot in apartments sitting right next to million-dollar homes.

Once, just a few weeks ago, a guy I'll call Frank left me a desperate note on the door of his apartment building. "Gone to dentist. Left door unlocked. Please leave my food." Please was written in huge bold letters. Frank's one-room apartment was at the top of the stairs, across yards of filthy carpeting, and the varnish was falling off of his door it was so old. I knocked first and then went in. Oh my. A sagging bed. One chair. Nothing on the walls. No photos of grandchildren. No wedding certificate. No black bedroom slippers resting gently next to the bathroom shower.

Inside of the refrigerator, there was nothing to eat. *Nada.* Zip. Just a few packages of catsup and a container that had like two peas in it. I couldn't help myself and so I opened three cupboards in his make-believe kitchen. One box of cereal and a few bowls.

I found out later that Frank walked a mile on the weekends to the McDonald's down the street where they would give him free hamburgers. Then he would sit by the window and wait for the Monday noon meal like a starving deer in the middle of winter.

The other guy down the block, we'll call him Harvey, lived in a house that I could smell from the street. Honest to God. Usually Harvey answered the door with spit on his chin, urine stains all over his pants, and his hungry hands reaching for the food.

One day he would not come to the door. Oh, shit. I knocked and knocked. I looked for a neighbor to help me but they were all at their real jobs, and then I walked around to the living room window and pressed my nose against it to see if he was lying dead on top of his card table.

It looked like a homeless shelter under the railroad trestle. Socks on the floor. Garbage piled up. Stacks of old newspapers and magazines piled everywhere. His bed was the worst. The sheets were rotten. Layer after layer of filmy black edges. Little holes where his butt must have rested were brown and frayed, and the layers must have been fourteen inches deep. Years and years of rot and filth.

He finally came to the door but he was obviously sick. He was as yellow as a block of cheddar cheese and stooped more than ever and his eyes were dark circles that were vacant and as deep as his last layer of skin. "No heat," he coughed at me. "Warming myself by the oven."

I raced back to the office and told Judy to get him the hell out of there. "He's really sick," I told her. She explained about the rules and how he had a social worker and there were no living relatives. We called anyway. They came and got him that afternoon and he died a week later in the hospital.

There also was the lady who was chain smoking while she was on oxygen. I could hear her coughing before I turned off my car and then that scrape, scrape, scrape of her tank being pulled along her cold floor and a wave of white smoke that trickled like deadly gas from underneath her door. That's the closest I ever came to getting blown up.

Another lady, not much older than I am, and riddled with diabetes, would walk her blind self to the door by moving her fingers along her paper-thin walls. I could hear her coming from the lobby—tap, tap, tap. One woman loved it when I brought my daughter. Rachel would stand still so the woman could run her arthritic fingers through her hair and then down the sides of her cheeks. "So pretty," she would say over and over again until Rachel shifted and gave me that, "Help me, Mom" look.

There were others. All memorable and then there was the guy we will call Hank who sometimes got stuck on the toilet. Such a flirt he was. Calling from his living room chair and asking me to get this and that so I would brush by his chair.

The only time I've ever had large breasts was the day before I gave birth to each one of my two children who set weight records, well, I set a weight record myself. What a little hog I was. I hated to disappoint Hank so I tried to push my shoulders together and bend low when I was near him so he would get at least a partial thrill. Cleavage is cleavage no matter how small the crack.

He had his chair placed so he could look out on the beautiful lake that he had lived on for the past fifty years. Someone came in to help him get into bed, clean his little toilet, and make sure he had some breakfast but mostly he sat in the chair watching Lawrence Welk reruns and remembering how busy the house had been when his wife was alive and there were always kids coming over.

"We had good times," he told me. "It was always like a big party."

I could just imagine and I wonder how many neighbor women old Hank squeezed in the ass when they come over to drop off cookies and the Avon samples. Such a naughty boy.

Because everyone on my route was always hungry it was impossible to spend much time with these food- and people-starved men and women. I'd stay as long as I could until I thought I heard the next guy's stomach gurgle.

Hank tried to think of many ways to keep me in the house. I got him some milk. I picked up the newspaper. I checked to see if there was a fork on the counter. I shifted a stack of books. At least I have a nice looking ass and my legs seemed to be holding up nicely. Too bad Hank was a breast boy.

Judy told me he was something like close to ninety years old and was holding out until he couldn't get on the toilet any longer. Getting off apparently didn't count.

Hank must have been able to tell that I was a party girl. He joked about drinking, and kept telling me about parties and the days when the lake was alive with real fishermen and people were always stopping by. "It was like living in a bar," he said with his bright eyes sparking. "Is that heaven or what?"

Each week Hank was kind enough to not get stuck on the toilet. Well, maybe I was a little disappointed because I knew he would be able to bury his head in my little mounds of flesh if I had to scoop him off there. I hated to deprive him of one simple little pleasure when there seemed to be so few left for the old guy.

One week, when my father was visiting I asked him to join me on my weekly Meals rounds. I thought this would also be a good time for Hank to get jammed up on the john, but when we pulled into the driveway, and I pushed open the screen door, which was never locked, he was waiting for me.

"Hank, it's Kris," I hollered. "I'm bringing a guest."

"Come on in, honey."

"It's my dad. He wanted to see this old joint and the fisherman who lives here."

The boys talked about walleyes and worms and whiskey while I loaded his food into the fridge and lined up his snack. Many of these people, Hank included, skipped lunch so they could eat the meal I brought for dinner. Hank always ate a piece of bread and had me put his meal away for later.

Back in the living room, the men were going at it. The stories were flying like hot tar in the July sun.

"Hey," Hank said, "why don't you guys go downstairs and see what's down there?"

My mind was swirling. The basement? Dismembered bodies? Old Meals on Wheels drivers? Dead worms? What in the hell could it be?

My dad hopped up and we slithered over to the basement steps. I put my hand on his arm and whispered, "Cripes, I'm glad you're here, Pa. What in the world could be down here?"

"Would you go down here alone?"

"Well, what do you think?"

"I think that most of the time you're nuts."

"It runs in the family."

The basement was a bar. A full-fledged saloon with signs on the walls and a little deck with a view of the lake and a bar that swung from one wall to the next. There was a line of leather-bottomed barstools and behind the bar was every conceivable kind of liquor that had ever been distilled.

"Wow."

"Oh, I bet that old fart has some real pissers down here," my dad said smiling.

There was a huge oak table where I imagine everyone played cards. Bowls for popcorn and chips. Chairs arranged in little circles. It looked as if someone had swept up, turned off the lights, and walked away just a few minutes ago.

Back upstairs Hank was waiting with a big smile on his face.

"What do you think?"

"It's great, Hank. I bet you had some parties down there."

"Oh, yes."

"Do you ever go down there?"

"Once in a while I get someone to carry me down the steps and I sit and look at it. It used to really be something."

Hank didn't want us to carry him down for a peek. The remembering and talking had worn him out like an old pancake. I bet he had to go to the bathroom. But I closed my eyes while I finished my business and I saw him swaggering behind the bar with a Camel between his lips and ice cubes glistening under those Budweiser bar lights. I saw him winking at the babe with the red lipstick and slipping the young neighbor boys a few beers.

His legs were wobbly when I shifted his chair just before we left and I bent down while my dad walked toward the door and I kissed Hank right on the lips. It was a juicy kiss that told him I knew about the good times and it was a promise that I would hold up the traditions of this hot papa as long as I could make it on and off the toilet by myself.

The Friend I Never Met Because They Killed Her

There is blood everywhere. Absolutely everywhere. It looks like someone slaughtered something right by the door and then dragged it into the tiny kitchen. There is also a pool of blood there on the cold linoleum floor by the old table that fans out in waves and covers so much space I think it is unlikely there was any blood left in the body.

I am looking and looking at everything and already I can tell what happened. I see where they pounded her head against the wall by the door and how she slid down to the floor. I imagine her hands covering her face and then moving to try and stop the fists. The blows came fast after that because she fought and because she was screaming for her baby. My God. The baby.

The hall is a short little thing that stretches beyond the kitchen and leads to two bedrooms and a bathroom. Only one bedroom interests me and it is where they found the baby. I can feel my heart rise like it is on the swell of a huge wave. It is pounding faster and faster, and moving beyond my chest and beyond any place that I have ever felt before in my life.

The crib is small and covered with blankets and sheets, placed there fresh off the line, scented with mountain winds, by the woman who died on the kitchen floor. The crib is empty now and the baby gone so fast to heaven with her spirit lifted on the fingertips of a speeding angel.

But this. This beautiful baby girl lying like a sleeping angel herself with her feet pushed out and her arms tucked under her belly—just like my own babies years from now and miles from this wretched place. There is only a tiny red line that moves from one ear to the next. It is where her uncle took the knife and pulled it across her throat from ear to ear so the little girl would die.

I watched the police video of this scene so many times I memorized every single thing I saw. I spent hours with the forensic men and women who helped me figure out what the last minutes of these two lives must have been like. We could account for every drop of blood, every bruise on her body, the minutes before the cord was wrapped around her swollen neck, her arm stretching toward the baby's room.

It was only much later, when my own baby girl was the same age as little Erica, the baby who died, that I came close to understanding how it might feel to know that your brother-in-law is going to kill you and then walk down the hall to slit the throat of your baby daughter. Much, much later and then how could I know? How could anyone ever, really dare to know?

But first I had to figure all of this out. I had to sift through files and talk to people who were inconsolable, and then I had to travel thousands of miles to talk to the men and women who knew this was always a possibility and that it could have been them.

Through months and months of it, I came to know Brenda—the mother on the kitchen floor—as if she had been my best friend. Her dreams and desires flooded my senses, and I knew how she sat and what she liked to eat and how frightened she was about her own marriage to the brother of these terrible men.

I walked through her yard and ran my fingers on the edges of the sheets and baby clothes that were hanging near the tipped-over wash basket. The hardest part was listening to the sound of her voice and the baby's voice on tape recordings. My throat would seize up when I tried to listen for those tiny squeaks and when Brenda would say, "Honey, careful," or "Good girl," I would have to blot out the sound by putting my hands over my ears.

It took years for me to stop waking up in the middle of the night because I thought I heard a baby crying for help. I think now that it was Brenda who cried for help because the baby would have known the face of her uncle, the killer, and she would have smiled to see him, hovering there above her white crib. It was Brenda I heard. Always Brenda.

It went on and on like this as I investigated these horrific murders, and so many people cried in my arms during my search for the truth, and then one day I drove to see Brenda's mother and father.

The windswept prairies of Idaho were not the kind of embrace I wanted on a trip that was taking me into the heart of misery. I wanted towering oaks and rolling meadows and spring flowers. Not the bare potato fields and the sagebrush that whipped at my car tires and the anxiety that came with not knowing what might happen and how much agony I would have to get through before I could touch a heart and hand.

I worried for nothing and I should have known because I knew Brenda so well by then—like mother, like daughter. Her mother embraced me right away and took my hand, and we talked while my eyes drifted toward all those photographs of Brenda and baby Erica on the off-white living room walls. Then I had to ask a hard question.

"Will you take me to the cemetery where they are buried?"

"Oh," said her mother, thinking, I am sure, about the one hundred other times she had already been there.

"I can go alone, you don't have to come. I just thought, well, we could talk a little out there and you could tell me about the burial."

She wants to go. I'm certain she would sleep out there if she could, and I follow her truck through the mud puddles and out past the edge of this sleepy town to a hilly area where the cemetery moves like a somber greeting from one edge of swaying corn to the next.

We walk slowly through the field and past the other grave markers. It is windy. It is always windy here and our hair blows around our faces and I can feel it cutting into me like a hundred little knives.

"I like coming here," she tells me. "It's quiet and I can work on my forgiveness and I can think about things."

"I think that's okay. You know, to come here as often as you want. It always makes you feel closer somehow."

"Have you lost people you love?"

"Oh yes. But not like this. This is beyond anything I have experienced. I can't imagine it, I just don't know how you ever get through it."

"It takes time and prayer, and there are hours to wonder and grieve. There's lots of that, Kris, lots of it."

There is no grave marker because Brenda's husband has used the money for something else. Brenda's mom points to the one burial plot and tells me they are both there.

"Both?"

I am not ready to hear this but it is a fact that will pull this story into the circle that it was meant to be. It will say everything to the world and it will say everything about Brenda and who she was.

"No one knows this but I think Brenda would like you to know."

"I feel so close to her. Please don't take that wrong but all this work to get to know her makes me feel as if we were somehow friends or at least we should have been. It's a connection. Some kind of connection."

We let the wind and the silence catch up with us as she prepares to tell me this startling fact.

"We buried Brenda and the baby together. We put the baby in her arms and we put them together. In there."

There is no way not to cry, and I grab for the mother of these two babies and hold her against my chest as the wind caresses us on this majestic plain of life. I feel her heart pounding and she is also crying and there, right below us, Brenda is holding Erica in her arms.

There were times, years after this, when my own baby girl would cry and I would shift my heart back to the days when I came to know Brenda. How odd to call someone a friend whom you have never met, but we did meet in the most terrible possible fashion.

So when my daughter Rachel cried I always ran to her. I ran fast and I held her for weeks and months until I could teach her about being strong, and then I had to slowly explain about how the real world works and how sometimes fate can play a cruel and inhumane trick on all of us.

But mostly, even now, I continue to love my own daughter with a fierce determination that shows the world they will have to climb over me first before they get to her. Just like Brenda. Brave, wonderful Brenda.

But Geraldo's Head Is So Damn Big

The New York air hangs like a bad dream over the miles and miles of concrete and bright lights and cars moving like lost geese and me carrying my little bag with the red dress that I will wear tomorrow on the Geraldo Show.

I am a woman of the world but such a country gal at heart it's a wonder I do not smell like cow shit as I'm riding toward my destination. The cab driver smells something about me and tells me to be careful because that dumb-ass Geraldo has put me up in a bad hotel where it is dangerous to walk outside after noon.

Great. Here's my big fling in the city and no one in the hotel understands what the word "iron" means, a cup of coffee costs forty-nine dollars, and there are frigging rats in my bathroom. This glamour stuff is not all it's cracked up to be.

I have written a book about a murder and this is the stuff Geraldo loves. But this does not make me feel good when I get up at two a.m. to stuff towels under the door because the man next door, who obviously has emphysema and lung cancer and no manners, is smoking so much there are flames coming out from under his door.

Geraldo forgets to give me money for breakfast. I am a poor woman with two children married to a schoolteacher and breakfast in the big city costs the equivalent of three gallons of milk, a loaf of bread, a box of Cheerios, and two suckers. Everything I do eat tastes like dog food. This is a trend that has not yet made its way to Wisconsin but I'll be watching for it if I get out of this city alive.

Before the taping I am off to see a producer who wants to make a movie based on my book. This is pretty darn good news for a woman who is the queen of story hour and lets her children eat lunch naked under the kitchen table.

Francine, the producer, is taken aback by my Midwestern charm and ability to just be myself. She also thinks it was smart of me to wear a red dress that will make my blue eyes flash and cause the TV cameraman to focus on the bright color. I'm not as dumb as I smell.

I would love to take her on a road trip where she cannot wear makeup and where people buy us pickled eggs and cheap beer when we stop at a tavern for lunch. I'd show her places where people live in trailers that are leaning into the northern winds and then I'd take her to my house so she could see my cute little office and the computer that is headed for a museum.

Her office is as large as half of my house and in her bathroom she has bottles of expensive perfume that would pay most of my son's college tuition. When I look in the mirror I laugh out loud because I can't believe I am in a producer's office in New York City.

I like to hike and drive on roads where I can just pull over and pee in the ditch. An exotic evening for me is a cheap bottle of wine and a movie with some great sex that is absolutely not like real life. Most of the time I would rather be writing than breathing. But, what the hell, the big city is a trip.

Francine is nice and I like her. She gives me a beautiful silk scarf with chairs on it because I am doing so many talk shows. This scarf will stay with me the rest of my life. I sent her some things in the mail expecting nothing in return and I think she thought that was kind of neat. I can't help but wonder if she's ever cooked bratwurst and watched the stars in the backyard past midnight. She is kind to me and although the movie will never get made, I also get to fly to Los Angeles and meet with CBS big shots and dance with a drunken man and pick the brain of a screenwriter and buy the kids gifts that will take me four months to pay off when the Visa bill comes.

My Geraldo show also features the last man who escaped from the grotesque arms of mass murderer Jeffrey Dahmer. Great. Before us a group of Nazis are taping a show that erupts into a fight. This is New York. Oh baby.

By the time Geraldo gets to the room where we are all waiting, I have been elected to tell him he's a shit. The hotel rooms suck. No one received food money and what's up with that? I try and act tactful but he looks shocked. And his head is so much larger than any other part of his body, and even though he has on cowboy boots, I am towering over him like a giant redwood.

He never sends us any of the money he owes us but the trade-off is that we get to spend the rest of our lives telling people how many wives he has had and about that head of his. It's worth every penny.

The taping of the show is a lot of fun. I say outlandish things so they focus on me and I remember to keep my legs crossed. When it's time to leave, all the men have to pee so I hold their briefcases in the hall and then ride to the airport with the Dahmer guy, a private detective, and some attorney. They cannot believe their good luck.

Flying back through thick clouds and one time zone, I remember what my father taught me. He always said to be myself and he reminded me all the time that I could be and do anything that I wanted to be. His life was sprinkled with lost dreams and hard work and standing at the window each morning with war memories that kept him awake. He was a wonderful father and his advice was the best advice anyone ever gave to me, and it is advice that I will plant in the brains of my own two children.

My babies come running when they see me and they want to know about the big city and about movie stars and taxicabs and rats in the room and what did I eat for breakfast? All the important things.

When I hold them in my lap I think of all the stories I have yet to tell them and about how one day they will fly off and set the world into a tilt that could change something very important. Someday I will take them to New York and we'll eat hot dogs on the street and go to the museums and wave at the Statue of Liberty. When we come back home, to our little house that will never be paid for, we'll be so glad to be back home, we'll make a fire in July and cuddle under a blanket.

But first, I have to tell them about Geraldo's head because it's just so damn big. Wait, let me get the scarf off first. The one with the chairs on it. It's from New York and it's very elegant.

Drowning in Lava Falls

There is something more than alarming about being two minutes away from drowning in the Colorado River. The water is up to my collarbone and I am still standing in the raft and people are screaming and we are being slowly sucked down into the bowels of the mighty river, and this is not how I planned to spend my thirtieth birthday.

It really looks as if you are in the middle of a draining sink when your boat tips just a bit and you hit the big drop wrong and the experienced boatman cannot row out of it and then you swirl and swirl and sink just a little faster with each turn until the water has covered everything but your face.

I came to this spot in the river as a soul searcher facing a monumental birthday and thinking about which road to travel next. I bravely signed up for the river trip alone and drove my little blue sports car to St. George, Utah where I zoomed past retired couples and memories of past trips that clung to me like rotten underwear. Some of my layers had to go but I had no idea what to strip off first, what to save, who I was.

It was September and my birthday on the eighteenth would be spent miles from telephone lines and deadlines and relationships that were beginning to smell like stinking cheese. Time for a change. A pause for a cause. An adventure. The sparkle of desert nights on my bare skin.

Everyone on the trip, it seemed, was searching through a million grains of sand for something they had dropped, something they had never seen, something they would recognize the minute they saw it.

My God the searching was fun and wild and wonderful. Sweet Virginia took me aside that first day because she liked me and told me she was supposed to be mourning her dead husband. "Really, I'm happy as hell," she whispered to me when I showed her how to use the bathroom in the wilderness. "He was a bastard and for the first time in my life I feel free."

We had to whisper because her brother-in-law was on the trip and he liked her dead husband. He also liked me and kept fondling my legs when I walked past him and talked about his wife with great affection. Finally he could not contain himself any longer and kissed me when I was going for my predinner wine. Virginia was on to something when she said the words bastard and men in the same sentence.

There were two couples from the East, a tiny little man who never stopped smiling and always wore a green Army hat, a boatman who had decided years ago not to bathe or use anything that might make him smell good, and the owner of the boat company who should have known better than to let this group of crazy people come together.

For days we drifted along the bottom of the canyon and dragged our bottles of gin and vodka behind the boats in plastic containers. We hiked up canyons, and sat up until the wee hours of the morning talking about cheap sex and the wars and where we had come from and had yet to go. The couples usually paired off early and the rest of us sorry losers sat up and poked sticks into the fire and drank out of our tin cups and listened for those ancient whispers to come riding on the heels of dawn.

I tried my damnedest to get Virginia to go skinny-dipping, but she thought going to the bathroom in the outdoors was a great first step, so I worked on perfecting her stifled laugh instead.

The actual day of my thirtieth birthday I was the only woman who wanted to go on a megahike that took us miles and miles up a canyon and then straight through a set of cliffs that would kill most normal people. It was grueling and beautiful, and then at my own party I was so exhausted from the hike, and more than a bit of vodka, that I had to crawl on my hands and knees through the wet sand to my tent because I could not get up.

Another person would have taken that as a bad start on the next decade of a life. Not me. I thought it was fun and cool, and even though my knees and ankles ached for forty-eight hours, I would do it again in a heartbeat—except not quite as much vodka.

Life down there below conscious normality danced into one beautiful experience after another. Soaring birds and the echoes of someone ancient calling from miles away and sleeping on the warm sand and bathing in mud as thick as bricks and bonds of friendship that can only be forged in places where everything is equal and where hearts are held in hands and where one morning you may be in water up to your neck.

On another hike we had to run-walk to a beautiful waterfall in order to keep on schedule, and I remember coming out of what seemed like a boxed-in canyon to see water the color of turquoise and pools that swirled in froth and the smell of ferns and what it felt like when I fell into the water and those miles of sweat were rinsed away. It was like a baptism of my wilderness spirit. Then running and running back to catch the boats.

Many nights, exhausted, I still could not sleep and heard Virginia out rummaging in the sand. I looked out of the little mesh window in my solitary tent and she would always be sitting with her back against a rock with her head pointed toward the moon. Freedom looked very lovely on her and I hoped the rest of her life would bring her some happiness.

My own happiness was usually just around the next corner and I never did reach any magnificent life-changing conclusions those fourteen nights I perched on the edge of the river. Mostly, I had a hell of a good time, which is really the biggest lesson of all.

When we got to Canyon Ranch there was a telephone hanging like a free-beer sign on the side of the lodge and on the spur of the moment I called my mother at work.

"I'm at the bottom of the Grand Canyon."

"What?"

"I'm on a river trip and there is a phone and I'm at the bottom of the Grand Canyon."

"Be careful."

It's not *not dangerous* to do this kind of a trip. People die down here. Boats flip. People get hung up in the rocks. They hit their heads and pass out, and then suck in water until their lungs fill and they sink and they become one with the river.

I tried to play it a little safe just to see how it felt and that's why I decided to hop into Mark, the owner's, boat the day we were set to run Lava Falls. It's a big sucker of a falls and dangerous and the kind of rapids you can hear in Toledo if you hold your head in the right position.

We pulled our rafts over to the large rocks that had fallen off the cliffs just to the right of the falls so we could get a good look before we plunged into them. I crawled over boulders the size of my house, and heard a deep churning and a rumble that sounded as if the Earth was burping. The roar was so loud we had to shout at each other and I mostly watched the two oarsmen to see who turned the palest. They talked and moved their hands, and then were silent for a long time as their eyes followed the waves, the covered storm under the water, the bulging rocks that could be uprooted at any second.

It looked like the stinky oarsman was the most apprehensive. He was usually not very quiet, but I watched him observe the waves with grave concern and I took this as a sign of frailty instead of as the mark of a man who knows his match when he sees and hears it. I chose to go with Mark, whom I later would affectionately call Flipper.

Running a river is a science and an art. Most people who row boats are nuts and should be on medication. They are addicted to a lifestyle that gives them days and days and days in this incredible canyon. These guides learn to read the river like we read maps, but the river changes. It changes from minute to minute, and if it rains or someone releases some water below the dam—forget it. You are on your own, baby.

Several times on this trip we had seen things floating past our camps. Things like empty boats. Oars. Socks. Pants. Food bags. Most of these occurrences were followed by boats filled with screaming passengers who had that deer in the headlights startled look that meant, "What the hell am I doing here?"

Well, that's part of the charm. Nature is a glorious beast and who knows what can happen tomorrow or just after dinner. For us, it was Lava Falls. The roaring devil.

We came into the falls from the right side and I held on to the ropes with the certainty that my life depended on it. Mark pulled hard to get us to the center of the river—the tiny spot where the waves form a V and will allow you to shoot over the tops of about 5,000 years' worth of silt and debris.

It looked like we were going to make it but then the boat turned just a little bit too much to the right and before any of us could move we were sucked into a wave that pushed us into a swirling mass of water the size of Alaska. That's how we came to be sinking and drowning in the Colorado River in the middle of the Grand Canyon.

First, I was worried about Virginia but she was holding on like a son of a bitch, and Mark was telling us to bail, bail, bail, and get some water out of the boat so he could pop us out, and little things were flashing through my mind. Things like my mother's voice and my dog's bark and how much I loved writing, and then it was bail, bail, bail, and I thought about going home for Christmas and how my family always seemed so glad to see me, and bail, bail, bail, and everything I wanted to do with my life that I had not yet tried, and bail, bail, bail, how would I ever unlock the secrets of my heart if I died in this fucking river that I had come to love and that was now treating me like just another pretty face?

We were caught in a swirl above some rocks and waves were spraying and I could hear boulders the size of small homes rotating on the river bottom and the deafening sounds of surging water slamming off one side of the canyon and then the next.

We were swirling in circles and with each rotation of the boat we sunk just a little bit deeper. First our ankles, then our calves, then our knees, hips, stomachs. I could not believe that I was actually standing in a boat and there was water up to my chin. This presents some unique bailing challenges.

When we finally popped out it was about as close to an orgasmic experience that you can have without actually having sex. We screamed and hollered and Mark got us over to the side of the river where we jumped up and down and hugged each other and cried and hugged some more and thanked God that we were not sucked down just one more inch, which would have made it impossible for us to get out of there without taking our chances by jumping out of the boat and into the unforgiving river.

On other trips I have flipped boats, and on one all-women trip we all rode down a serious succession of rapids in lingerie and when we rounded the corner a group of bare-chested men about fainted when they saw us float past in garter belts, strapless bras, and thin-laced nighties. Lava Falls took the cake as far as heart-wrenching experiences go.

I think it is interesting how some memorable adventures seem to grow brighter as the days pass. It has been seventeen years since I took that river trip, and I can close my eyes now and tell you what we had for dinner Thursday night and the color of the boats and how the moon slid from behind the red rocks one night like some magic wand from heaven and made every single one of us drop whatever we were holding.

Now when I am close to being sucked into some void of life that threatens to extinguish the tiny river flame I keep burning inside of me, I can often pull out of the swirl by using sheer willpower. The sky, you know, is really not so far away.

It is a powerful feeling to know that you can save yourself, and that the forces of the world and the people and places inside of it can be held back by the magic of the human spirit.

I've Fallen and I Can't Get Up

There is one window just beyond the little cell in this white emergency room that lets me see the waving hands of the Hawaiian palm trees. The kids are out there building forts with dead branches and making the most out of something that has now turned into a whole new kind of experience.

I am bending up and down and helping my elderly friend who has fallen in the sand on the first day of her long-awaited vacation.

I am cleaning her shoes and her underwear and I am watching her grimace in pain and I am thinking about how this was not part of the plan. Not at all. We were just supposed to get her to Hawaii before she got too sick and old.

I am talking to the nurses and hoping the doctor is not a jackass because my friend is one tough old bird who was a nurse and probably could turn this goddamn hospital upside down in about twelve minutes.

I am also looking into her Irish eyes and seeing all the years of her life flood onto the sheets like a river of pain. Her life is bleeding out like a worn out song and this "I've fallen in the sand" event is the single movement that has pushed her over the edge.

Later, when we help her up the steps and I bathe her and bring her food, and then we spend quiet days helping her walk and shifting her legs and moving just that one slow inch at a time, I will listen as she tells me her life story.

She talks because the dam was somehow jarred loose when she fell and there is no stopping her now. She likes the way I tell people to go to hell and how I do my own thing, so she trusts that our hearts have always flown in the same direction. She talks until I nod off in the dark and then she starts all over again when I pour the milk on her cereal hours and hours later.

As the stories build into a moment that has reached way beyond the doors and has filled the living room and the long porch and is now moving toward the Pacific Ocean, I see a sparkle spread from one of her eyes to the next until she realizes suddenly that, "By God, I've had a life."

Forget the pineapples and the fruit drinks and walking through the sand, I tell her. I hold up the mirror, and she sees all the stories floating past her and she sees that she has covered more ground then one-hundred marauding camels and she has written her own book of rules and she has seen the sun rise in Mexico and set in the Mississippi swamps.

Before we take her home I will sneak off to the beach by myself and plant my feet half in and half out of the swirling water. I will throw my dried flowers, the lei of hope, into the highest wave and watch as it drifts to the farthest corner by the rocks and struggles to get back out into the open water. It is still there, fighting like a son of a bitch when I turn to face the rest of my life.

Already I see my wish coming true and thousands of nights of adventure erasing the word "no" from the slate where I store my guidelines, and then I am walking naked on a thin line of wire that stretches around the world and touches hearts and smiles at the storms, and never, ever do I look back but always ahead.

Always.

The Little Girl and the Tomatoes

The sun is so hot I want to throw up. I can feel my breakfast bubbling at the edge of my stomach and I have to close my eyes, focus with all of my might, keep my feet squared on the ground, and not breathe to keep that food down there where it will help me grow.

It is my first day as a tomato picker and it is ninety-five degrees and I am thirteen years old and making one dollar an hour. This is a big deal. My brother started working at the Bass farm last summer, and I waited and waited for my birthday so I could stand there with him and fry my brains out.

Not just anyone can work here. You have to prove yourself because this little town is riddled with kids who want to do this. We all want the money and something to do and it's better than babysitting for fifty cents an hour.

My brother, Jeff, is no help at all. He just says "pick" and doesn't give me any hints about how to do that. The Radish kids are no slouches. The nuns like to pick on us because we all have big mouths, especially me. But our dad works seventy hours a week as a brick mason so we can eat dinner seven nights a week. We are workers and beer drinkers and we are tough as nails. We know how to cut the mustard and pick the tomatoes.

Picking started at seven a.m., and the first hour was easy and almost at the far edge of fun. My hands are working faster and faster, searching for the tomatoes that are almost ripe. There is such a difference between the really ripe tomatoes that will sit at the stand at the edge of the road and all the other little tomatoes that will be boxed and sent to grocery stores and end up in homes where people actually have things like air conditioning and automatic ice-cube makers. You have to pick just the right ones for the right box.

By eight a.m. the smell of ripe, gushed-out tomatoes is getting to me. It gets hotter and hotter, and I know only one thing that no one else but Jeff knows.

"If you pick good and don't puke, she'll let you stay and pack and that's like the best. So don't puke."

This is not so easy. There are three more hours to pick, and my hands are sore and my back hurts already and I want to throw up so badly it hurts to breathe.

But I will not throw up. I will not. I will eat it if it comes out. I will put it in my pocket, brush it through my hair, stand on it, but I will not really puke.

Just before noon Mrs. Bass comes out into the fields and she is smiling. I have always loved Mrs. Bass even before this because my father who volunteers with the St. Vincent DePaul Society tells me she has a boy in her house who is full grown like a man but who lives in a crib. She changes his diapers and rocks him and feeds him because he is still her baby. She only goes right to town and back, and she watches over him and says to people it is not a burden and that he is her son. Damn it. Her son.

This is what I think about as she walks toward me. She looks and is so tiny, and I am already inches above her and everyone else my age— "a tall broad" is what my father calls me. I can't imagine her changing the diaper because the boy must be so huge but I am young, still so young.

"Kris," she asks me, "can you stay and pack?"

Oh my God.

I have done it. I have not puked and I get to stay and Jeff stays and so does Lori, her granddaughter. This is like the proudest moment of my life. Jeff doesn't even care. His mind is always in the woods. He already walks like the bowlegged logger he will turn out to be.

Packing is not as easy as I think it will be because now all the tomatoes are in one spot. There are hundreds of them and the way I wanted to puke before is nothing like the way I want to puke now. It is a desperate longing that surges and surges about every ten seconds.

I will not eat tomatoes for years and years after this migrant-worker experience but one day, when I am in my twenties, I will pick up a tomato and it will speak to me. It will talk about not giving up and going the distance and getting what you want, even if it just about makes you puke in front of Mrs. Bass.

That afternoon my mother makes us stand in the backyard because we stink and because we have mud and dirt from our ears to our little butt holes. She sprays us and sprays us, and I will not let go of the six dollars that I am squeezing in my hand.

One day I will use those six dollars to help pay my own way through college. I will work three jobs at once, carry a full load of classes, be the editor of the campus newspaper, and be on the dean's list, and I will do it all by myself. I will travel the world and sleep in ditches and love men and women, and two babies will spring from my loins. I will write books and be on television and dance naked in more places than I can remember.

But nothing will ever feel as good as that six dollars in my hand and the mud running down my legs and my breakfast still there making me grow into a woman and my mother who always, always loved me so much, laughing as the water squirts her in the eyes back in the summer sun in 1967 in Big Bend, Wisconsin.

Traveling North

Rachel has barely finished her nursing at Mama's breast when she pulls on my leg to ask me, "Where are you going again, Mommy?"

"I'm flying in an airplane to Canada to see the woman who is in jail, you know, the one I am writing a book about."

Rachel has her daddy's hazel eyes and hair so blonde it almost disappears into her own pale skin. When I look at her, I think that she must have been switched at birth. She is so beautiful. She wants me to go away like she wants the flu.

"Don't go—k?"

I have not gone anywhere for so long I barely remember how to drive.

"Oh, honey, this is mommy's job and I'm here all the time and it will just be a few days, ok?"

"No."

Rachel will be like this every day of her life. She will always know what she thinks is right and what she wants and needs, and she will never let anyone get away with anything.

I go anyway because I have to. Not just for this woman behind bars but for Rachel and for myself. Rachel and her brother Andrew will grow up with visions of their mother on the phone talking to people in strange places and me always at the computer and scraps of paper up and down the hall and manuscript rejections that pile so high we could burn down a barn with them.

They will always know that I love them. They will also know that my work, which is part of my very soul, is something that I need to sustain every other part of my body.

So I go and they wave from Grandma's arms and suddenly I have gone from diapers and Bert and Ernie (oh who cares if they are gay—at least they are happy) to the gates of a foreign prison where a woman with holes in her socks is pouring her heart out to me in the waiting room.

"It's cold in there," she tells me, constantly working her fingers at the edge of her worn-out jacket. "They all get sick. Everyone gets sick."

"This is my first visit here."

"It looks good now from this spot but it's not good. Not good."

I am guessing prostitution might have landed her in this waiting room as I look at the lines on her face and her hair stripped of every natural color. Her female lover got caught selling her body, and now she is alone and sitting in a prison waiting room.

"I'm sorry."

She looks surprised when I say this, and she reaches out to touch me and then pulls back as if I have given her an electric shock.

When she looks away I touch her with the tips of my fingers in that little space between wrist and arm where the coat never quite reaches. Then she watches me leave as they call my name and I slip into the bosom of the women's detention center in Toronto, Canada.

My friend looks like hell. She is sick. The woman out there was right. She has lost weight, and her eyes have black circles the size of bottle bottoms and her hair hangs in clumps that tangle where they meet.

"Jesus Christ, the fans blow all night, and I'm on the top bunk and I just have this measly sweatshirt."

The worlds I step in and out of are so different that it is a wonder I do not employ a staff psychiatrist. One day I am breeding children and throwing bad waffles to the birds in the backyard and then, zip, I am sitting with a greasy prison phone in my hand while a convicted murderer slips forward in her chair.

"Everything is different up here. Everything."

We talk and talk, and she puts her fingers to the window and that is how we touch. I show her the book cover that has her photo on it and what I have written in the beginning, and we could fill up all the spaces of a month with words if we only had the time.

Clearly, there are things about me that she will never reach in and touch. She will never know what it is like to have your son sleep with your nightgown because he misses your smell when you are flying in an airplane to Canada. She will not know what it is like to hand off the crying baby to a husband because you are on a deadline so tight there is not time to turn off a light. She will never know what it is like to have to take a collect phone call from prison knowing that you will never be able to pay for it and that your daughter will have to poop in your hand while you are talking because you can't get her to the bathroom.

And me? In this world of steel bars and monitors in the toilets and strip searches and food that tastes like it has been dragged behind a car—do I really know anything of this? Anything?

So we talk in increasingly loud tones until I hear keys jangle and they push on the edge of her chair and she has to go, and when she stands up I see that she is as thin as a person can get and still be alive.

The woman in the lobby is gone, and later that night as I walk the streets of Toronto and throw a good-night kiss to the Wisconsin stars, I think about how some lives are always on the edge, prepared to fall, tinkering with the sockets that connect them to their own lifelines.

I think about what it would be like to spend ten years in prison, to escape through the laundry room, work as a waitress, and then end up in a foreign jail.

I think about so many things my head hurts and I wonder what the hell I am doing here and then I look down at my own fingers. These are the fingers where the words ease out like soft folds of paper onto my computer screen. These are the hands that touch the hearts and souls of the people who come begging to have their stories told—the people with other gifts—and I have this gift of writing and turning a movement as simple as a muted sigh into an exclamation of delight.

Later, when I have been back to the prison for another fast conversation and have flown home to the dancing delight of my children, I remember that professor who almost drove me insane with Bs until I pulled myself up to the crest of the mountain by my fingertips and saw a world formed by writing perfection that might just one day be within my own grasp.

I thought of him and treks to prison that seemed to wear down my heart and soul, and then behind my eyes a rumbling started that was the cough of all the people who have yet to have their stories told. I put Rachel down for her nap while Andrew was at school and I wrote without breathing until my daughter was at my knee and asking, "Where are you going next, Mommy?"

Oh My Susie

The day I found out Susie died I had been working in the hospital coffee shop. Driving home through the city, past the edge of the apartment complexes and into the country, I could roll my window down and breathe something that smelled better than the thirty-five cheeseburgers I had just cooked.

I liked the drive home. We lived in the country and it gave me time to think, to jingle the tips in my pocket, to imagine what I could do with the few free hours of my life that hectic first year of college.

My mother, I know now, was pacing all day as she waited for me. She realized what she was about to face when I walked in the door. It is a gift, really, to be older now myself and to imagine in the clearest sense what really happened during the last twenty minutes of my innocence.

She would have prayed while she was pacing. My mother always prays. Even now, I never call in the morning when she is reading her prayer cards and fingering the white rosary she has misplaced about three hundred times. That particular day she would have been on her knees, too, planning and searching for a way to tell me that my best friend, my cousin, my soul sister, had been killed in a car accident.

It was not a pretty scene when she told me. It was however, a single, crucial, changing-me-forever moment in my life. I could not, would not, believe it. My mother tried to touch me, wanting I suppose, to let me accept the warmth of her hands, an embrace, anything she could offer.

"It must be a mistake," I shouted. "Mom," I yelled, screaming with such force that she stepped back, "this is wrong."

But it was not wrong. There was gravel on the side of the road. A misplaced tire. An accident. One horrible moment. Susie hitting her head on the seat and then her soul flying away before the car stopped, before a heart could skip a beat, before the blink of an eye.

I was inconsolable. I raged. This level of sorrow and hurt was as unfamiliar to me then, when I was so young, and no one, no friend, no family member could help me.

Susie and I were more than just friends and cousins. We had been raised together, three houses apart and the six months difference in our ages was nothing compared to the thousands of hours we were together. We looked like sisters. A couple of tall broads who told people where to stick it. We had been raised by two of the wild, tall, fun-loving Radish brothers—our dads, Bobbie and Dickie—who settled scores with their fists, but had hearts that were as soft as silk.

Susie and I had so many plans. We were young, restless, and full of ideas that even now seem impossible. I was in college and Susie was in technical school and we wanted to head west. So many plans and dreams and then the sudden collapse of the world into a reality as harsh as—death, only death.

My father tried so hard to help me. He had been a soldier in the war and he knew more than I will ever know about fleeting moments and the sacredness of every second of our lives. But, he

173

could not help me. I was in a dark spiral that even today seems like a hellish nightmare that could not be stopped.

Finally, I wrote, which has always been solace for my weakening heart. It was a tribute to her, to us, and I took my little tribute down to the newspaper where I also worked. Everyone knew about her death, because the story about the accident had been in the newspaper, but no one there could help me either. I was a fugitive searching for the killer of my own heart.

When I could not put it off any longer I went to see Uncle Bob. Her daddy. His wound was twice the size of mine and I watched in pained shock as this man, as large as anyone I have ever known, fell to the floor sobbing uncontrollably.

There was no end to our grief. The funeral and the wind blowing in off the river and the priest leaning in to touch my elbow. "You will see her again, Kris, really, I know it." I believed him and there was comfort—for a time.

I spent hours at her grave. We talked there, Susie and I, and I prayed more than I ever have before or since. I would sit with my back to the fields, my hand winding the tall grass in and out of my fingers, and I would try and make sense out of what had happened.

None of us were ever the same. It ruined all the days and nights of my aunt and uncle's lives, and because Susie and I looked like sisters, it was almost unbearable to visit them. My aunt would stare until her lip twitched and she had twisted off the last inch of her fingernails, and I would always end up in the bathroom crying.

More than once, when they were downstairs, I slipped into Susie's room and was overwhelmed by the smell of her. I felt the edges of her bed and ran my hands along the side of her dresser and looked at the photos of her hanging on the wall.

I wanted something, anything, from her and didn't know yet, back then, how much of her was already inside my heart. It would take years for me to simply grow silent when my grief would resurrect itself like a bad word, rising from my toes and pushing through my stomach, past my heart, and into my mouth so quickly that it left me dizzy.

The paralyzing grip of grief could happen anywhere and it did. At meetings, in school, at parties. It was so goddamn hard to go on without her and no one knew what to say to me.

There are times, even now, when a thought of her is like a slap that brings me to my knees. I will see something or remember a time, a moment, the way she always seemed to appear when I needed her, and it will disarm my emotions. Then, oh then, I know what I have of Susie. It is a memory of a time, those times, all the times that our hearts crossed and we shared the precious joy of friendship and love.

I am a grown woman now who continues to mark my days and years and events by comparing them with what Susie might have done, who she might be, what she would have done, what she might look like with gray hair and bags under her eyes like mine.

Often I wonder if our children would have been friends and if our own friendship would have survived all the comings and goings I used to tie my life together. Would she really have left with me when I headed to the mountains? Would she still laugh like a mad dog when we talked on the phone? Would anyone still turn their heads when they saw us, so tall, walking into the bar?

I cannot forget her and that is her legacy to my wounded heart. When her parents stare at me now, I let them because I am a mother now, too, and I can only imagine how magnified my own grief would be if my daughter, Rachel, or my son, Andrew were to befall the same fate as their Susie.

It has been years since I visited her gravesite, mostly because I realized it was not that place, but what had once been, that lured me toward that black, granite rock that marked her gravesite. Now, I can talk to her anywhere. It doesn't have to be in the fast-filling graveyard. I will never stop missing her. It is like a chain that seems to tighten just a bit when a year and then another passes.

It has been twenty-eight years since she died and I think the greatest gift in this tragedy is how it prepared me for the string of losses and sorrow that linked together all the other days and nights of my life.

When I thought that I could not go on, could not handle it, could not bear to see that side of life for another moment, I could turn my head, just an inch, and see my heart, impaled on the sword of grief that news of her death brought to me. It made everything easier—eventually.

Now that I have tempered the lining of my heart with the wisdom that comes with age, I see her as she was and remember the feel of her hand on my shoulder, the weight of her legs as we fell asleep on the living room floor, the sugar cubes that she passed to me on that one birthday, her giant laugh echoing from three houses away.

And my grief remains one of her greatest gifts to me. It is a touchstone filled with the realities of life, with the truth that maybe it is not so silly to eat, drink, and be merry, with the consuming knowledge that I really will see her again, with the knowledge that she never really left.

I've Picked Out My Husband's New Wife

This idea came from where? That's what I want to know as I sit in front of this tiny ranch house where the woman is dying and is willing to tell me what it is like to know, almost to the minute, when she will say a last good-bye to her two children and her husband, and allow her disease to triumph because she can no longer fight it. Not any longer. Just a few days. Maybe a week.

I have already interviewed an elderly man who has had a life to match all lives and who has been to war, and made love to his wife hundreds of times, and held his grandbabies, and once traveled by airplane to Europe where he watched his wife smile for fifteen days in a row.

There was also a little boy with a head so large and filled to the brim with so much fluid that he walked around the halls of his home with padding covering his shoulders so when he fell over he would not get hurt any worse than he already was. His mother trailed after him in constant fear. The counters were littered with medicine bottles and notes, and there were towels on the floor because he might get sick any second. All he wanted to do was run, just a little bit, one or two more times.

This woman was the last one I had to talk to for this series that I thought was such a bright idea before I actually had to write the damn thing. Stories about people who knew they were going to die. "Well," I told the editor, "it happens all the time and it might help people to know what it's like." He thought so too and here I am finally, finally at the last interview, and what could I have possibly been thinking?

A man answers the door who is one of the city planners on my government beat. I know him and yet I didn't know about his wife. I feel my teeth drop into the sides of my shoes.

"I didn't know she was your wife."

"I didn't know how to tell you."

"Is it still okay for me to do this?"

"Oh, yes, she wants to talk to you. This is very important to her. It will be okay."

This man has a weary look that speaks volumes about long nights and medical bills and a life that has been turned upside down and will never be the same.

Someone has taken great pains to make the house neat and tidy, and he explains that he does not want to be there when she talks to me.

"I just came home for lunch."

"Okay."

"She may get really sick when you are here and if that happens call this number and her friend will come over right away. They are very close friends and she will know what to do."

"Okay."

"Also, if she needs something quick she will show you where the pills are."

"Okay."

She can no longer get out of bed and she tells me this right away. Her room was probably once their room and it is now the hospital room of the house because she wants to die at home.

These are the last walls she will ever see. This is what I think about as I move into the room and see her thin face, eyes that are puffy, tubes and towels, and this tiny pair of pink slippers sitting just to the left side of the bed.

I feel like such an intruder and I am more than embarrassed. But this woman has so much dignity and so much poise, even in these last hours of her life that she manages to make me feel comfortable and worthwhile.

"If you believe in God and heaven and life after death it does make it easier," she tells me. "People never talk about these things as much as they should."

That is no problem for us. We talk and talk, and she tells me about her pain and about the cancer and how it snuck up when she had her head turned and grabbed her by the throat. From that second, the day she knew, her thoughts were only for everyone else. Never for her, because in her mind she was already gone and the saving now, well, that had to be for those who were left.

I will never be this strong. That is the thought that is rambling inside of my head. Never. I will curl up in a ball and cry and order expensive booze and then throw myself off the roof.

"There is a calmness that comes."

"Really?"

"Everything falls into place and you know that it's okay."

"What about your family?"

"Oh, they will be fine," she says, as a cough moves from her chest and passes above each rib until she is unable to speak, because the cough is in charge of everything.

"Can I do something?"

"No. Listen, though. I've picked out my husband's new wife."

What? What? What? This question is pounding from one side of my head to the next but we can't talk any longer because she has been seized by the pain. It has grabbed her and it is choking the life out of her as I watch.

I run to call the number and the woman is there before I can hang up. She is there because she knew. She must know everything. She runs past me and I can see in her eyes that her life is focused on this dying woman. Just her. No one else.

There is a flurry of movement and pills and something to drink, and I watch quietly from the next room. These two women talk and hold hands, and it is clear that they love each other very much. I know then when I see the neighbor woman touch the dying woman's face and bend on her knee and then bury her head into the sheets while she waits for the medicine to work. I know that this is the woman who is supposed to marry the widower.

It is clear that the interview is over. It is clear that they need to be alone.

"Thank you," I whisper into the dying woman's ear. "Thank you for everything."

She turns her head and looks at me, and her eyes are clear and strong, and she smiles, which must take a great amount of effort.

"I like your husband's new wife," I tell her. "It looks to me like you have really good taste."

Her smile grows a little bit wider and I tell her friend not to get up, to please stay right there, and then I leave and when I do I lean against the door with all of my weight and I think about how terrible it is to live in a world where society is so slow to change how it feels about love and relationships. I think that in another time and place this dying woman could maybe love her husband and her friend and if that could happen they could also find a cure for her cancer.

Then I drive away and I think of the women in that room, holding hands, whispering about the light on the mountains and how the dying woman's little boy likes to have his pajamas tucked under his pillow. They are remembering the Thanksgiving when they ate hamburgers instead of turkey and the time they walked downtown and ate lunch at that new restaurant.

I don't know if that woman ever married her friend's husband. But when I think about her, and what could have and never did happen with her own life, I remember what my mother told me one day as we were looking at her high-school photos. I kept asking her what had happened to this person and that person, and she had no idea.

These were my little-girl years when my friends swayed in and out of my life like bending reeds and when I was in love with all of them and when I knew, right here in my heart, that they would be part of my life forever and ever.

"What?"

"I don't know where any of them are now."

"Well, they were your friends. I don't get it."

"Oh honey," my mother told me. "You will be lucky if you have one good friend in your whole life. That's all you need. Just one."

Just one. One to help you through those last days. One to touch your heart and to be there, kneeling at the edge of your bed. One who will hold you and know everything about you and then comfort you as you lie dying on an afternoon in late spring just before the trees bud and there is still snow on the mountain that you can see from the bed in the middle of the room.

Jan Graham's Bra

Driving home, my then-husband wants to know if I noticed Jan Graham's bra straps. He is the kindest man I have ever known in my life and when he fell in love with me it was a sound that I could actually hear. It was as if someone dropped a pan of marbles onto the concrete floor, and they bounced and bounced and then they all somehow managed to roll into one spot and that was right at the edge of my feet.

Well, I did notice her bra straps. They crossed in the middle of her back and I was sure when I saw her tight calves that she must be a runner and that her bra would keep her all in one place as she ran during her lunch break.

This is not really what we need to be talking about but there is no place to begin a conversation that could change the course of our lives.

Down below my seatbelt there is a big baby boy kicking the living hell out of my uterus. To the left of us the Wasatch Mountains are beginning to twinkle as the cliff dwellers slowly turn on their lights. On the other side of the highway I can see the faint edges of Utah Lake but now I can't stop thinking about Jan Graham's bra.

"Do you have a bra like that?" he asks me.

"These days, in case you haven't noticed, I'm wearing a hammock. I will never be able to wear a bra again."

"Oh, sure you will."

"I need a wheelbarrow just to get to work."

"Well, I know you will be able to wear a bra like that. I liked it quite a lot."

"I liked it too. I'll see what I can do."

My husband knows I don't get mad when he looks at other women because I look at them also. Women always look at other women but I am one of the few women who love women and men and can admit to this old-as-the-world fact.

Today, though, I don't much care about Ms. Graham's bra because she has given us some startling news. This is what we are avoiding by talking about bras.

She thinks I have a chance to win a discrimination suit against the people who now give me a paycheck each week. She tells me it will not be a pretty scene and that we will have to fight in court like brave warriors but she said the facts are the facts and the main fact is that what they are doing to me is wrong.

The wrong stems from several issues that will someday be a book themselves. But the basic details are easy to understand—at least for me. I should be able to write a book about a murder I covered for the newspaper on my own time. I should be able to tell the truth, the whole truth, and nothing but the truth. I should also be able to work without being sexually harassed.

"It's up to you," she tells me while my husband sits in the chair and watches her bra straps. "I've taken this to everyone in the firm and they think we can do it."

I am eventually planning on leaving this state but this will change everything, and I am angry and pissed off and disgusted and have never been one to back away from a fight. But there is so much to consider. My life is as complicated, I mistakenly think, as it will ever get. I am pregnant. I am planning on moving to Wisconsin. I am a wild woman who cannot be stopped or suppressed.

My list of grievances having to do with my employers stretches out for four or five years, and now I have this new complaint that includes religious freedom, personal rights, and a woman's basic need not to be told anything asinine by a man.

My husband and I begin to talk about what we should do very slowly and finally he lets me make the decision. This is a good thing because I am usually fierce in my convictions—even if they are not always perfect. This also means I will be moving into a quiet place while I think and where my love for everything and everyone will have to rest until I decide. This is a huge, life-changing decision and it really is something that I must decide alone. Even as I dive off the cliff, forgetting to make certain the water is deep enough and the rocks are cleared away, here I go.

Do I file a lawsuit or just forget about it and leave?

So it is up to me. One thing that could happen if I decide to stay and pick up my weapons to fight these people is that I will have the baby by myself while my husband returns to Wisconsin. This was not how we planned any of this but that's life, isn't it? You make this nice plan to drive fast through the mountains and suddenly there is a huge mudslide that changes everything.

I spend hours driving up the canyons and waddling to my favorite spot on the creek where I buried my cancer-ridden dog. I talk to the wind and I ask the nature goddesses to help me. I only hear a slight screeching from inside my own mind when I wait for an answer and then the baby kicks again and I fall over because his feet are getting so damned big.

This land has made me weary. That is one thing I do know. I have had to fight for every inch of ground that I have covered. I have had to beg for every raise and have had to prove myself twice and then twice more because I do not have a penis. I have had to use every ounce of patience and understanding that I possess to be able to keep pace with minds that will never really accept me for who I am and that will always be hoping, so it seems, to baptize me and save my wretched little soul.

I understand that I work for a newspaper that is owned by The Church of Jesus Christ of the Latter-Day Saints or the Mormons, but I also understand that they don't own me just because they pay me to work for them. When I think of all of this I think that I cannot do it any longer. I think that I owe this baby every drop of myself and that I will need all my energy to bring this child out of my womb and into a world like what? A world like this where censorship and a patriarchal society can even touch someone like me? No thank you.

When I call to tell Jan that I can't fight any longer, she is very quiet on the end of the phone, and I do not even think about her bra straps. She understands, she tells me, because she is also tired.

Leaving is not as simple as it sounds because years of my life are stacked up here and the geography of this country has bonded with every breath that I take. I have loved so many things about my job and the people I have met and taken into my heart. There have been great adventures and challenges mixed in with all the sadness. It will not be a picnic when I leave and it will take me years to make my new home a place where I can rest my heart easily and without regret.

We leave and drive across the country and sleep in our little tent, and I am so huge that one night I get stuck in the zipper on the way to the bathroom and end up peeing under the light where everyone can see me. Everything is harder than I thought it would be. I try and put the decision to leave and not file the lawsuit behind me and with each mile I am hoping that it will fall into the dust behind the wheels of our new blue truck.

But it never does. I have this baby and he is so big they have to cut him out of me. Then I begin this new life, which is absolutely nothing like my old life, and I think about the decision and about all the women whom I could have helped and I sob in the basement when Andrew, my son, is sleeping because I don't want his baby psyche to hear my failings.

Years pass and I am so sick of myself I wish I could take it all back and start over in Jan Graham's office. I would even buy her a new bra. I would go jogging with her. Anything.

There is another baby then and it is a girl who slides sideways out of me because from the very beginning she wants to take the world by surprise and she has legs like a giraffe that rip me from chest to bone to spine when she storms into the world.

That is when it gets really bad. When I look into her hazel eyes I see that I have been an ass by taking the easy way out, which has turned into the hard way after all. I think of what I will have to tell her one day when she stands in front of me with her hands on her hips and says, "What kind of wimp are you anyway, Mother? You left without filing the lawsuit?"

This eats at me until I think I will crawl on my hands and knees back to Utah so I can sacrifice myself in front of all the women who have been wronged since I left. I could have stopped it. I could have made a difference. There is no way to comfort my spirit. I feel as if they have won again and some days it is hard to walk.

Then there is a miracle. I hear about another woman who has fallen under the same spell at the same church-owned newspaper and I think this may be a chance to redeem myself and make amends. I send her a letter and tell her that she is not alone and that I will help her by sharing my story if I can. I am fearless and I am also a mother now, and that changes everything. Absolutely everything.

"You will?" she screeches in astonishment, because I find out that all the other women are scared and afraid to step out of the large closet that will propel them into another world.

So I tell my story and leave nothing out, and this woman, who also has a baby growing inside of her, she calls me and weeps on the phone and says she will never be able to repay me.

"Oh, you have already repaid me," I say. "I have found my lost soul."

My new friend gets a little money from her settlement but she gets more than that. She wins, and I'm not certain, but I think some of the people who don't win must think about equality and freedom of choice and acceptance and how change is a good thing and about how it's wrong to think you can control the world from just one spot on Earth. I hope they know it was me who broke the spell and took a step forward.

Sometimes I still talk about Jan Graham's bra and I have started running again so that I can catch up with all those other pieces of myself that I left behind that day I decided not to stand with the sword in my clenched fist.

The friend I helped also calls me brave and tells me she owes me the world but I know better. We all owe each other the world and silence is not a very good way to pay off our debts.

Then there was the unbelievable day when her daughter and my daughter held hands and swung their feet on the bench by the restaurant, and I looked into their eyes and into the eyes of my friend and I felt that I had redeemed myself and that maybe, just for a little while, I could stop running so goddamned hard.

Eskimos on the Cliff

Mike falls backwards off the cliff and for that second, when I see his feet punch the sky and his arms disappear into the black night and then his voice like a hollow pleading, my heart stops beating and a line of panic races itself up my leg, through my stomach, and into my throat.

My then-husband and Jim, the winter guide, rush to find him while I grab the kids and huddle with them against the fire, protecting them, I think, from something that is grotesque and horrible.

The miracle of the ice is alive and well. Mike has caught his foot on a frozen tree root on the way down and is suspended between the icy, rocky ledges of Lake Superior and the top of the cliff.

"He's okay," shouts Jim. "It's going to be okay."

For crying out loud. We are fifteen miles from civilization and camped on a tiny island in Lake Superior. I'm writing a magazine story about winter camping after being pulled into the wilderness by a dogsled team. There is not a cloud in the sky and there are stars blinking across the horizon that you can only see in a place like this where there is no haze and the air is an unbleached layer of gauze that shifts with the pure North winds. In just a few hours it will be way below zero and nothing we do will keep us warm in our nylon tent, under sleeping bags, wool blankets, and seventeen layers of clothing.

But first we have to get Mike up the side of the cliff and assess the damage. He is groaning and he cannot walk, and we put him on the edge of the picnic table and see what we can do.

"Do you want to go to the hospital?"

This is a very complicated question. We have arrived on the island via dogsled. There are two packs of dogs sleeping below us and it will take us, at the very least, one hour to hook them up and begin the journey to that little speck of light we see in the distance.

Then we would have to decide who would go and who would stay. Then the people who stayed would have to figure out how to get off the island if Jim stayed at the hospital with Mike.

This winter adventure has definitely turned into a drama. But Mike says he thinks he will make it. His leg is already swelling like a balloon, and I save the day with my flask of brandy and the pain pills I have in my little backpack.

We manage to get Mike into his tent and then we huddle by the fire and reenact the grisly scene for a good hour. Mike is talking to Mr. Brain, my son, and he is so engrossed in the conversation that he doesn't remember he is standing on the edge of the cliff. His arms are crossed and just as he moves his right hand into the air to make a point, he steps backwards. It is just a tiny step but when he puts his foot down there is nothing there. Nothing but that black space. Then he falls and we think his brains must be splattered across the beautiful white landscape. It takes ten seconds. That's all and then the wind shifts through the trees.

Somewhere north, just beyond the next island, we suddenly hear something howling. This is so perfect I want to fling myself off the cliff like Mike did. Wolves? Maybe. Probably a coyote, Jim tells us. We hear the dogs stir and one by one they also begin to howl until there is a chorus of growling and deep-throated whining, and Jim finally tells every last dog to hit the hay and then he goes and sleeps with them.

I don't want to go to the tent. Once, back in my old life, I was cross-country skiing and backpacking in Yellowstone National Park and I became a crazed fool who got hypothermia. I love winter and being outside but since that night, when my teeth chattered and I saw little kittens with red dresses flying through the sky, I have been terrified of freezing to death in my tent. Also, this is one of those moments and places that I never want to forget. I want to drag out every second so it seems like an eternity—no matter how damn cold I am getting sitting on this rock that feels like a huge ice cube.

We have mushed across the ice with the winter sun in our eyes and sipped hot chocolate while dancing to keep our toes warm and jumped over open leads of water that made me close my eyes and say a Hail Mary and rounded the corner of the island to see miles and miles of drifting snow and shifting ice and pine trees leaning over to touch their necks to one open spot of water.

I have watched my babies' eyes dance with delight as they guided the sleds and stood on the runners and cried, "Yee-haw." Then I sat with my head resting against a warm blanket and I let my hand dip in and out of the glimmering snow as we pushed from one side to the other around the edge of the island, searching for the perfect campsite away from the wind, and where we could find lots of firewood.

This is like a dream. A magical adventure that stretches through two days and shows my family that life is always and forever about pushing yourself to see what is around the next corner and never worrying about staying dry or keeping your head covered because the feel of the air, the wind, the snow on all those places is more than a perfect experience.

When there is just enough wood left for the morning fire, I poke the coals into a little pile and then head toward the tent. My God it is cold and Andrew is dead asleep in his preadolescent coma while my daughter, Rachel, clings to me as if I am the inside of a furnace.

We are bears in a cave and, of course, my bladder that has carried the weight of two large babies cannot make it until morning and now, in the heart of the night, it is so cold that you could stick pins in my frozen head and I would not feel them. Then, like clockwork, Rachel has to pee really, really badly the moment I am back in the tent, just the second I feel a spot of warmth creeping slowly up my arm.

Mike is alive in the morning and he has taken to hopping instead of walking. He drags his cameras and his four hundred and fifty rolls of film with him, and we pack up the rest of his stuff and begin the incredibly complicated job of hitching up the dogs that are so strong I can barely hold on while we unwrap the harnesses.

Then there are those hours of mushing when I can think of accidents and living on the edge and the luck of the draw and handing my children all the choices of the world and men falling off of cliffs. And of course we decide to take the side roads on the way home and stay off the freeway because isn't it the journey? Isn't the journey the whole deal? Absolutely every damn thing is the journey and the most important thing of all.

Savage, Savage Hearts

After all those months of working so hard to get the women's shelter opened up, I am stuck on the one life that we could not save. It is the woman who was blasted with a shotgun in the foyer of her own home. The man who shot her walked the children over her dead body so he could drive off to nowhere.

And today there is yet another domestic violence murder on the front page that includes nineteen blasts from an assault rifle while the victim cowered in a boarded-up home because he was going to kill her and she knew it and no one would help her.

It seems endless and senseless, and today's murder reminds me yet again of the woman in the foyer who we also couldn't reach and help.

I am with a police officer who is sitting across from me in his detective's office with an open folder of photos of the foyer murder scene. I want to write a story about her and make her life worth something, if only it is to save someone else. My fingers are tapping lightly against my notebook and I am trying to remember if I saw this woman we couldn't save. Did I see her at the grocery store or at the movies or just walking down the highway because she lived three blocks from my house?

She is familiar, maybe because all women are familiar to another woman. Women in distress are drawn to other women too, because they know at least another woman will believe and understand. And maybe once she caught my eye. Maybe I was driving past as she was at the 7-11 and she raised her eyes and she was really screaming, "Save me," and this is what I heard but I kept on driving.

When I go to my board meetings at the women's center, I think that it is a miracle, a flipping miracle, that we have finally opened the doors to the hidden crime of domestic violence. In this place where anything bad is covered with a white blanket so it blends with everything else, this one thing—spouse abuse—it is rarely spoken of or acknowledged.

But from the day we opened the doors, the beds are full and the women keep coming, and their men drive around in their Dodge pickups getting angrier and angrier because they do not know how to find us.

But this one woman I want to write about never made it to the shelter. She called. We know that because the woman who runs our shelter has her name and she shows it to me like the secret that it is and we put our heads on the table and ask each other over and over again, "What if she had come over that day? What if ...? What if ...? What if?"

So the detective thinks I need to be prepared to see this, and I look at him and his little moustache and I say thank you very much but this is nothing. I have seen more than you will ever see, sucker. I want to know where he was when she tried to get someone to keep him away. I want to know why the woman we have in the hospital with her brain swelled up and pushing against every bone in her face had to crawl to the street before someone finally took him away. I want to know where the son-of-a-bitching gene comes from that makes men crack bones when they hear the words, "No, I won't do that anymore."

The detective is trying to be kind. I realize this so I let him off easy. I also know that he takes his daughter hiking and that when he talks about his wife it is with a degree of love and affection that means she is his equal. He is definitely a wise guy.

In the photos he shows me, the slain woman is lying with her back against the wall, and with her arm trailing up the steps of her little trilevel. Her feet are spread about thirteen inches apart and she is sprawled just as she fell when the shotgun blasted her almost in half.

I know what she was thinking. I know how she had already seen this happening and how she was worried, always worried about the kids and never enough about her own self. I know how she hunched in the corner of the bedroom with a kitchen knife in her hands and how she crawled on her belly down the halls in the dark on that green carpeting the nights she saw him parked out there watching for a shadow against the blank window.

I know that she talked to her friend in Salt Lake City who had no more tears left when I came to see her. I know how parents and those make-believe ministers kept telling her to hang in there and give it another try.

I also know that she knew she was going to die. When she opened the door in the middle of the day and there he was with the gun and she moved her eyes from those deep holes where his eyes used to be and down to the gun, she knew that she was going to die before she could blink.

Making the kids walk over the body is so unforgivable that I think it is a shame they did not give the man who murdered her three life sentences because the kids are ruined now also. "Is Mom okay?" they must have asked him and then the pool of blood by the big green plant and her hair matted with specks of red and the daughter looking over her shoulder for Mommy, always looking for Mommy.

He wanted the children to visit him in prison after all of this, and the shelter director and I are heartsick because there isn't anything we can do. We have already done what we can, and the beds are full and they will always be full.

The detective watches me as I thumb through the photos and I find this a total invasion of my privacy. I do not let one muscle of my face move or one tear drop or one finger flinch when I see the autopsy photos and all those pictures of what she looked like those years before him when she was so damn happy.

It is so fucking hard not to be angry at the world when I work on stories like this. I manage to say thank you. I am like a drunk with all these feelings making me woozy and it is unsafe for me to drive. I sit in the car for a long time and I wrestle with the images of her life and with the choices she made and with the tipped-over bicycle in her front yard that she could see as she fell over.

She was so close. Just an inch away from a new life with her school almost finished and this plan that she had shared with her friend in the city, and she had called the shelter, and yet she stayed for that one extra day and he killed her.

Unfortunately, this remains one of my unfinished stories. It is in a file that stays open on the top of my desk because I know there are more facts to gather and more cops to see and a pile of photos that never seems to diminish.

Now her babies are grown, and I imagine the grave has not seen fresh flowers for a long time and that the people who live in the house do not even know what happened there. But some of us remember and there are more than a few of us and the beds at the shelter are full but there is always room for one more if we can only make sure they have the phone number.

The Day We Almost Died

It is not supposed to happen like this. I want to be an old lady when I die, and have a Pulitzer Prize on the wall and books with my name on them lined up on the shelves. I want to see my daughter perform open-heart surgery and my son sit in the governor's chair. I do not want to fall from the fucking sky in this airplane while my husband tells me over and over again that he loves me and it will be okay.

How can this happen? I have been to war and people have fired guns at me and men have held my arms against the concrete walls in deserted warehouses and I have smashed cars and nearly drowned and have gone into hiding when bad men threatened my life.

Now I am on an airplane flying home from Grenada where my husband and I have been alone and away for the first time in so many years I did not know how to act for three or four days when there was no spilled spaghetti during dinner and no screams in the night because of the bad guy who lives in the closet.

Nothing has prepared me for this. Childbirth, rock climbing, swimming upstream, fighting evil with truth. Nothing has prepared me for these moments when the goddamn plane is flipping out of the sky and people are screaming and there is a chorus of Hail Mary's as we drop thousands of feet from one cloud to the next.

It is an Easter storm and the gods have sent these gusts of wind, rain, and sleet, and they are dumping water out of their clouds in buckets the size of the Empire State Building.

I know we are in trouble when I turn to see the stewardesses sitting in seats with their heads in their laps. Jesus Christ. This is the prayer that floats off my lips like nothing I have ever uttered in my past lives.

We drop and the plane holds for just a few seconds and we drop again, and then below us I see the lights of Chicago and I think to myself, "There is no way in hell he can land this plane." There are no other planes in the sky because they have been diverted to other airports where the sky does not have the face of a hurricane. But we have no gas. We have to land.

My hand is on my husband's arm like a claw hook. He will have bruises for a month and his arm will never be the same in those spots where I pull into his muscles and draw blood. Next to me women and men have their heads bowed in prayer and my life flashes, just like they say it does, and I see every moment that has ever been a part of my existence.

It is a swirl of colors and laughter and tiny hands and the divided energy of all the men and women and boys and girls whom I have loved. There are forests and mountains and a prairie that stretches from sky to Earth and everything is rotating like a never-ending movie.

Then we are so close to the ground that I see a few faces in the terminal and I let up for a minute. This is a bad thing because we are suddenly hit by a wind shear and then we are going down the runway sideways. Sideways. I see a man standing by the window and he is drinking a cup of coffee out of one of those paper cups and I am praying to God to make it quick so I will not have to hear my husband's last screams just before he dies and then I fall into his arms and follow him back into the clouds of hell.

We roll back where we are supposed to be and the pilot aborts the landing. Jesus Christ. Help us. Save us. Please God. Please.

Then we have to go back up. We have to go back up and do it all over again, and people are moaning now. There is a chorus of distress and sorrow that fills every inch of the cabin, and I am shaking and my hands are jumping and I will never fly in an airplane again the rest of my life. If I live. If I walk to the car and drive home and slam myself into the bodies of the children I will never leave again, not for one minute forever and ever.

We go up and up, and the pilot circles and I am thinking this man may have a connection. Maybe he knows an angel or this is his second chance. I hope so. I am praying for it.

We drop and drop again, and I imagine the pilot is trying to hold the plane in check like it is a loose bull. I think of his hands and the way his legs must be pulled around so he can brace himself against the instrument panel.

I can feel the wind. It is more than fierce. It is tossing the plane like it is nothing but a speck of dirt and it is pushing us down, too fast, too fast.

This second time around is worse because we know what is happening. Everyone is crying, and people who have never spoken to each other are holding hands and resting heads on unfamiliar shoulders.

I see my own life spread out again like the first time—it is a huge blanket that is blowing in the wind. I see all the people that I love and the places I have seen fluttering in the breeze, and I see my babies. My babies. Then that is all I can see or hear or think of—my Andrew and my Rachel.

We get closer again, and sweat is pouring from my face and my head is down and I have a death grip on the arm and I am trying to get ready for the crash. Trying but not succeeding.

Then there is the window again and the man with the coffee is gone and then I feel the wheels touch down and I begin to sob as I hear the brakes grab and we are on the ground and we are alive and people are clapping and crying and we have been saved and delivered.

The terminal is chaotic and we help people who are so weak with the lingering caress of fear they cannot walk. There are rosaries gripped in warm fingers and grown men stumbling, and some people drop to their knees and they cannot get up off the floor.

When I realize that I can walk myself, and that all those grandmas and grandpas are safe, I run to the phones to call my mother. "We are safe," I tell her and when I hear her voice, that echo of everything that I am and ever will be, I cannot speak. A wave of emotion washes through my heart and covers my entire being, and I cry from a place so deep and hard and secret that I do not recognize the sound of my own voice.

I cannot stop this, and finally hang up the phone, drop to the floor, and let it ride out of me. I am alive and my heart is a jagged flame that burns like a solid echo inside of me. I can feel the blood pounding through my arms, and legs, toward my eyes, and through every vein that connects in the maze that is me. I am breathing and alive and have been given a chance to continue to paw my way through life.

Staggering, I feel as if I have survived something so fierce and passionate that I may never recover and I never do recover. I avoid flying for years and when I finally get on a plane, I get stone drunk and cannot remember that I watched a movie and flirted with some man who slipped me his business card.

Once a fearless broad, I cringe when I see any airplane flying overhead and I feel as if some little knot that has never been tightened now has a stranglehold on my heaving insides. I am angry and frightened, and I change the way I think and the plans I make for travel and the very direction of my life.

This goes on and on until I fly again and my daughter catches me drinking vodka out of a water bottle in the bathroom when she accompanies me on a business trip to Florida. Then on another trip, where everyone tags along, my doctor friend gives me some happy pills, which make me want to fly by myself. That was a wonderful series of flights. If I could only remember where I went.

The point, I tell myself, is that I got on the airplane and I only threw up once, and we did not crash. I feel the knot slip just a little bit.

One afternoon, I am looking in the mirror and I see lines trailing out from my eyes and down my cheeks. I see dark bags under the first layer of bags under my eyes and new veins the color of plum pudding pushing out around my nose and my hair, just before the dye job, is the color of old snow. I am suddenly seized by the thought that I have always been fearless and it seems ridiculous to change when I am now so far and long into the program.

Well, I tell myself, grow up, you dipshit. So what if you have to get drunk to get on a plane. So what if the mechanics may be stoned or the pilot may be in the fourteenth hour of his flying day or a new wind may rise up out of nowhere and throw the plane into the side of the mountain.

It's not like I am ever going to forget that day I dug a hole in an arm. It's not like I am ever going to not cringe when I hear an airplane or when someone asks me to fly to Washington, D.C. to give a speech.

I don't care what anybody else says. It's okay to drink and fly, and to carry around a little pit of pain in the hollow of my stomach that erupts into a volcano when I feel that surge and we are flying.

Yes, there is no telling when a truck on the freeway might rear-end me or my heart might short-circuit or I might finally poison myself with my own cooking or fall onto a steak knife or slip off the bed and put out my eye.

Please pass the wine, I say, and up yours, and no I'm not going to that church anymore until women can be priests and they stop telling me how to vote and the whole world who to love and who not to love, and screw the idea of saving money for retirement, and why can't we open the window and scream at midnight, and sure have that candy for breakfast, and let's turn up the car radio and dance in the driveway, and if you wanna do that then what the hell, and get over it right now and kiss me, just like that, on the lips because we are living, we are definitely living and that means we are also flying—way up there—even if we are scared shitless and always will be.

We are flying.

The One Thing I Wanted

A bike. That is all I want. The only thing I want. I want it from the moment I get up in the morning until I fall asleep each night dreaming about it.

I am riding around my little village on a bicycle that was built before the Civil War. It has solid rubber tires and is a hand-me-down from Chris Nowak. It gets me from here to there but it is not my bike, it never has been, and it never will be.

Christmas of 1961 is my salvation. I have my Santa list prepared before Thanksgiving and it is glaring at the entire family from the refrigerator door.

I begin to pray for the bike. It is the miracle I need to turn me into a woman. To gain me some respect. To help me fly over the back roads and to school and across town when my mother runs out of butter and sends me to the store.

But in the back of my mind there is always this little frightened space that says my parents can't afford it. Christmas at our house is a glorious day that never centers around tons of gifts. We eat and go to the Radish party, and Santa comes but his bag is light when he gets to our house.

We always have enough to eat and my mother sews my clothes and we are not really poor but we are not even close to rich either.

Rich kids get new bikes right when they ask for them or maybe just a day or so later.

My cousin Susie has a bike just like the one I want and when I see her on it I can barely speak. It has white metal fenders and a seat with springs under it and handlebars that are silver and have white grips on the end. I love her bike so much. More than anything.

I am eight years old and taller than anyone else in my class except Susie and we know there are no girls in the world taller than us. We are friendly giants. The short girls have new bikes and Jeff Oakwood makes fun of me when he sees me round the corner pushing like I am racing from hell because the bike weighs as much as a small tank. He makes me sick to my stomach and I will show him when I get my new bike for Christmas.

My parents murmur behind my back and I think they are deciding what color to get. I cannot think the unimaginable—that they are trying to tell me how Santa doesn't have the money this year. Nope. Not that.

Christmas is very close and Grandpa and Grandma Goodreau are coming. My mother is cooking and cleaning, and we have the bed ready in the boys' room, and they will get to camp out with me because my baby sister is not even born yet and there is plenty of room.

I am so perfect during all these days that I know when I die I will be a saint. Saint Krissy. The one who got the new bike. She was perfect. Tall, but really perfect, they will say.

Christmas Eve is a big, big deal. My mom makes a turkey, and I pick at it and look out the window and worry about all the snow that keeps coming. Will Santa make it? Oh, Jesus, I pray over my mashed potatoes—please let him come with a bike.

After dinner we are allowed to roughhouse because we have to stay up for midnight mass. There is definitely no falling asleep. My grandparents are coming along, and Dad goes early because he is the usher and has to get things ready. I want to throw up because I am so nervous but that would ruin my saint status and so I force myself to stay calm. I am hours away from the bike. I can feel it.

Grandpa lingers in the house while we are waiting and waiting in the garage. My dad leaves and then comes back for us because we only have one car. When we get in the car he stays in the house a really long time. Finally he comes out and I never do see him wink at my mother.

This is the longest mass in the history of the world. It is way too long and I don't really give a crap but I can't say this because of the bike. My chapel veil rests slightly crooked on my head, and I ignore the way my brothers Jeff and Randy kick at the kneelers and believe I am like the nuns in the choir. Quiet. Thinking. Praying. Perfect.

It snows and snows, and when we leave mass there are huge chunks of snow that have to be moved with trucks in the parking lot. Wow. Not good biking weather but it's kind of neat and we will have a ball jumping off the roof on Christmas morning.

I cannot even talk in the car. Last year Santa came while we were at mass. Maybe this is a new trend. Maybe there are bike tracks in the snow outside the back door.

Now I am afraid to go into the house. Oh, what if there is no bike? My life will be ruined. Jeff and Randy are in there for a good five minutes before I can bear to walk into the house. They are yelling and I know what is happening.

I kick off my boots and set my jacket on the counter but I forget to take off my white winter gloves with little fake pearls on the cuffs. I walk into the living room like one of those June brides who takes little baby steps. La, la, la. I am in no hurry.

Grandpa has made a fire so the living room is glowing and when I open my eyes I see that there is no bike. Oh, my heart is hurling toward the floor and there are tears behind my eyes and I cannot think because my grandma keeps saying, "Kristy, go put your gloves in your bedroom."

She says this over and over, and finally I can't stand it and I run down the hall never intending to come back out the rest of my life. When I fling open the door I see a pink bike with metal fenders and a white seat and springs and everything I had ever hoped or dreamed for in the eight years of my life.

I cannot touch the bike or look at it because its beauty is blinding me and then I start to cry. There are just little sobs at first and then sobs that seem to grow as big as the three wise men until I drop to the floor and my mother rushes to my side and holds me there against her beautiful soft skin.

"Honey, honey, what's wrong? Don't you like the bike?"

I look up at my mother who has on a white Christmas apron, her green wool dress with the scoop collar, and her red lipstick. Always her red Avon lipstick.

My mother loves me so much I can feel it every day of my life. I look at her with tears running down my cheeks that pool in the hollow of my neck and I cry even harder.

"Oh Mommy, I'm so happy. The bike...."

Then she dips down, and I fly into her arms and I can see the bike, and it is the one thing I wanted, the one thing.

Years pass, dozens and dozens of years, and I always have a bike. I sometimes ride one hundred miles in one day. Whenever I see a little girl on a bike my heart dives like a sweet bird and I remember the bike I got when I was such a little girl. I remember it as if that Christmas was yesterday.

When life gets hard, when I sob in the corner for other reasons, when things seem impossible, I always think of the bike. I think about how I wanted it and then it came to me.

And I never ever stop thinking like this.

Never.

Daughter Love and Shopping

Prom-dress shopping is finally going to turn me into the alcoholic I was always meant to be. Give me a spoon so I can gouge out my own eyes and then eat them. Let me stick needles under my fingernails. Send me naked onto a large hunk of ice that is slowly melting off the frigid coast of Alaska.

Anything.

Anything but shopping. Anything but trying to find a junior prom dress for a girl who is about to become a woman and who may possibly lose her virginity after I purchase the dress.

Anything but standing in this dressing room where I, the mother, am wearing three-dollar flip-flops, a pair of shorts I found for next to nothing at the sporting goods store, and a very cool (so I think) bright-pink shirt that should have been thrown away twelve years ago.

Anything but this dress that she thinks is stunning, which it is, that will cost more than any single piece of clothing I have ever purchased for myself.

"It's three hundred dollars," I mouth from behind the tiny pieces of red fabric. "Three hundred dollars for less material than most everything I own."

"Mom, get serious," my absolutely stunning seventeen-year-old daughter advises. "A friend of mine just bought a dress that costs three times this much."

Like I give a shit, is what I want to, and do say. Like I care what anyone does or thinks, I also say. Like this other dress that has a small tear and we can get for forty-five bucks will not be just as lovely before you trip on it during something you call dancing and rip out all the seams.

My stomach is churning as if someone has dropped a lit match down my throat. I would actually rather eat flaming matches than shop with my daughter. My daughter, Rachel, who is fortunately, and unfortunately, almost six feet tall, beautiful, and in so damn many ways just like me.

"Let's see what everyone out there thinks," she says calling my bluff. "Let me walk out with this cheaper one on, and then the other one, and let's see what people think."

This is exactly what I would do and so I cannot say no. I would do just what she is doing and while she slips on the cheap dress I am suddenly paralyzed with the notion that she has turned into me and this is supposed to be a good thing.

Rachel puts on the dress and announces to the dozens of mothers and daughters, who are also shopping for prom dresses, that we need help. The first one, she says without hesitation, is nice, don't you think? They agree in sort of a stunned mutual nodding session. Their daughters are quiet and not like this brazen hussy in the blue dress.

Lovely Rachel flips back into the dressing room where I am praying to every goddess in the world that they will find the three hundred dollar dress just as ugly as my shirt and flip-flops. She puts it on as if it were a handmade glove. She slips into this dress with the open back and slits up the sides and low neck, and my heart stops. My daughter is drop-dead gorgeous. I am also thinking that once I looked like this and I am still pissed that no one ever noticed or told me.

She pulls back the curtains as if it is opening night and the crowd goes wild. These jackasses shopping for prom dresses actually clap. They love it, and her, and I bravely stick my head outside the curtain and see her, my baby daughter, with her arms tossed in the air and high-fiving all the girls and their damned mothers.

I think at this precise moment how I never went to prom. I think about how she may never go again. I think about how I will never have another daughter, another shopping moment like this, another wild-ass girl who will have a photo of herself in a beautiful red dress the rest of her life.

I buy the dress, which I cannot afford, and I swear to God and Buddha and every other thing and being that I will never again shop the rest of my life. I will order my bathing suits from Land's End and all my blouses from Chico's. My daughter can run naked for all I care. I will wear my clothes and make her wear her clothes until they rot off of our shoulders and drop to the sidewalk.

I HATE TO SHOP.

And my daughter, the model could be, loves it.

And as we drive home in the car, and she tenderly clutches the plastic wrap that is caressing her dress, she talks to me. She says, "Thank you, Mom." She tells me that she suddenly remembers I never went to prom and how I always say I don't care but how I probably did, back then anyway, because her friends who are not going are miserable. She talks to me. We move on to her class schedule, her on-again/off-again boyfriend, her latest level of pain during her period, the after-school job she hates, and then we are just quiet and she slips her hand onto my leg and when I feel the warmth moving from her long fingers into my thigh, I let go of an almost sob.

"Mom," she asks not faking concern, "are you okay?"

"I'm fine, just fine," I assure her hoping she does not take away her hand.

"You would tell me if there was ever something wrong, wouldn't you?"

"I think so," I respond trying not to break this spell, holding on to this moment so tightly that my toes ache.

"I hope so, Mom."

Then she lets out a sigh, and I turn and see her caressing what there is of her new dress and smiling and glowing from anticipation. I know she has probably never been happier than this moment and I am so glad I am with her that I can feel my heart speed up.

And this happiness is partly because we bought the dress she wanted, partly because she knows I hate to shop but did it anyway, and partly because well, we were just shopping and that is something she loves to do.

What have we become from shopping, this woman-to-be and I? How did we go from the little-shirt-trying-on session in the very first dressing room all those years ago, to this stunning performance at the mall? And most importantly—will our mother-daughter relationship survive and flourish or take a nosedive and vanish because of this commercial madness?

My lovely Rachel and I have been shopping together since before she was born. I remember balancing my wallet on what must have been her rear end as I tried on maternity clothes and then later as I held up outfits that were so tiny, so precious, so adorable, that it made me weep to imagine putting her feet inside of them.

After she was born, and I dared to go into a department store, it usually meant taking along her brother—who still shops at secondhand stores and loves to have his birthday clothes show up with discount tags and wrapped inside of used plastic bags.

Rachel was the kind of baby girl who would instinctively reach over and touch the most expensive article of clothing no matter what department we were in. She could pull out a high-end silk blouse as we were slowly walking past a display filled with a little of this and a little of that.

I was in trouble and she could not yet walk.

When she did walk, shopping became an adventure, an education, and often a hilarious tangle of questions that seemed to cover everything from bra straps to anatomy.

"Mommy, why do you put those things on your breasts?"

"To hold them up a little and because it just looks better."

"Mommy, are you going to have another baby in there or are you just fat?"

"Just fat, sweetie."

Those were the golden shopping years which were very quickly replaced by the *"I Hate You, Get Out of the Dressing Room, Do Not Look at My Breasts"* early-teenage years.

These were the years when I often cried as we went shopping because I was such an ignorant fool. Because I had no taste in clothes. Because I would not spend four thousand dollars for a pair of jeans and because I was losing a daughter to the almighty and immoral world of consumerism, and of course to her friends, and anyone else who did not look like a mother.

I am ashamed to admit that we often fought during those years. Not quiet fighting either but the kind of fighting where you think you are whispering but where you are really almost yelling and saying things that your mother once said to you like, "You will wear this or go naked." Or "Get a job and buy your own clothes, little Paris." Or "Do you think I raised you so that half your body parts could be on public display?"

Our bonding during those years was almost painfully absent until that one day when she allowed me to help her purchase a bra. It was not her first bra but it was her first real bra and it would have been wrong to cry during this passage but I so wanted to. It was tender and lovely, and as I helped her hook the back I forgave her for all those years of hate-filled shopping, for thinking that I was a fashion idiot, and for laughing at me when I honestly said that something made her look beyond foolish. Forgiving myself came much later.

This is when we started talking again, and when the questions started again, and when for a brief period of time, I loved shopping with my daughter.

Did I mention this was a very brief period of time?

"Mom, will I ever get real breasts like yours?"

"Honey, you have lovely breasts and someday they will grow a little and you will wish they had not."

"You have cleavage, Mom. I so want cleavage."

"This took over forty years to get, sweetheart," I responded proudly, lightly touching my breasts. "Be patient. You look like a model, you're tall and beautiful and apparently I was also. No one ever told me though."

"No one ever told you that you were pretty?"

"Not until I was something like forty-one," I admit.

"Oh, Mom, I think you are beautiful."

I was so absolutely happy during these kinds of moments that I almost, let me repeat that *almost,* thought I liked shopping.

We talked about everything in those dressing rooms. Drugs, sex, rock and roll, dance class, boys, exercise—there wasn't much we did not cover. After she got her period, there was a brief slice of time when she was once again shy and made me stand outside the door and flip things back and forth to her while she was in there groaning and talking to herself.

She was still growing into what would eventually be size-eleven shoes, and something disgusting like a size six or eight everything else, and finding pants and jeans to fit her five-foot-eleven-inch frame—which will never be easy. But we managed, and even as I learned how to bite down on my bottom lip as we paraded through stores so she could find whatever in the hell she was trying to find, I was happy to at least be with her.

Happy because she was beginning to not want to be with me, beginning to slip into the arms of her friends, beginning to realize that she knew how to shop alone and that it was more fun to do it without a mother who continues to wear flip-flops in the dead of winter, fleece year-round, and who cuts the sleeves off of all her T-shirts and loves to wear bandanas in her hair—in public nonetheless.

"Stop tucking things in for God's sake, mother," quickly became the mantra when we would go shopping. "And what's with the cowboy-belt fetish?"

As you can see the lovely days of mother-and-daughter shopping for new grade-school clothes quickly evaporated into her begging for rides to the mall so she could shop with her friends.

How dare she!

This was supposed to be our time and as much as I hated to shop, I missed the drives to the mall, or the local department store, and watching her face when I said "yes" to a purchase instead of "no."

It took a while, but right around prom-dress time she stopped asking for the money and started again asking if I would go with her.

To say I was flabbergasted is an understatement akin to nothing I can imagine or put into words.

"You want to shop again—with me?" I asked pointing to myself and clearly looking as if I was about to die of shock.

"Come on, it will be fun. We can have lunch and you can buy me things."

She laughed and at first I saw it as a trick that would help her get me to override the annual clothes budget. I was half right and half wrong.

We started talking again the first time we went shopping. She did want more clothes, and I met her halfway on that. And as I watched other people watching her, I realized that my born-savvy shopper of a daughter was now more than just that. Rachel had become a beautiful, confident, self-assured young woman.

A woman.

And she was woman enough to reach out as we strolled through the mall and hold my hand.

And she was woman enough to make me try on clothes that were impossible to tuck in but still not baggy.

And she was woman enough to tell me I was a fool for thinking that the clothes she wanted were not a necessity.

And she was woman enough to accept the fact that my budget did not always match her wants, needs, and tastes.

And she was woman enough to begin asking me how I felt, what I wanted, and for my advice.

This was and remains a true miracle to me. The transformation from little girl, to sweet preteen, to not-so-sweet teen, to this young woman who could go into a store, select several items, throw them together, and come out as if she were just leaving a *Vogue* cover shoot was almost too much for me.

Too much, but so lovely, because this is also when our shopping conversation changed from just talking about shopping to once again talking about everything. Perhaps it was the distraction of the shopping masses, or because she was in a venue that she was clearly comfortable inhabiting, or because she really had hit the "You Are Now a Woman" watermark. Most likely it was all of the above.

All of this made me want to shop with her again—occasionally. Please. I'm not insane enough to think that she'd still always rather be with me in a mall than with her best friends who have really become part of her posse and her own self-designed family.

In all of this the education and transformation for both of us has been rather simple. *Let her be herself.*

Rachel will always love to shop and will most likely always want to look stunning even if she is just going out to walk the dog. Fortunately for her, she looks stunning in my sleeveless T-shirts and old shorts, which she also has worn on occasion when all of her clothes are dirty, but to her credit not outside the house.

The mother, that would be me, will always not like to shop and I'm at that phase of my life where I can still look okay when I have to give a speech or sign books, but give me something made out of cotton that stretches and I'm singing like a wild bird.

Just after the prom dress had been flipped into the back of the closet, where I had predicted it would end up, the seasons were again changing and I could tell Rachel was gearing up to ask me for some summer clothes and we know what that means.

A trip to the mall.

I waited for weeks, and it got warmer and warmer, and then one evening, when I was sitting right here and writing, I heard a faint call from her terribly messy bedroom, which is just across the hall.

The noise picked up and I stopped typing.

"Mom," I heard her yelling.

"What already, I'm writing."

"Mom, get in here, quick."

"What?" I said almost tipping my chair over and wondering if her hair was on fire.

"It's online shopping."

Oh my God.

Online shopping.

No drive to the mall.

No long lines.

No incompetent sales people.

No worrying if there is a bar at the mall where I can get a drink in between the underwear store and buying her yet another pair of shoes.

I was so happy that my heart pushed toward my throat and I thought I might cry.

I got into bed next to her. We crossed our legs, hers on the bottom mine on the top. She leaned into me. We giggled. I went to get drinks from the kitchen. She showed me something. I said, "Too much." She kept looking and found something better and cheaper, and we high-fived.

We were shopping from her bed. She leaned into me and it reminded me of that time in the car when she touched my leg and I was gladly thinking I would buy her any damn thing she wanted.

I suddenly loved to shop like never before, and Rachel and I spent almost two hours shopping while in bed. I slipped in questions about her boyfriend—who is apparently on-again this week, if she has filled out the college applications, and what grade she thinks she will receive in the AP math final.

We shopped.

We laughed.

We bought.

We are finally two happy shoppers.

Please pass the computer.

I Will Always Be Their Mother

The father of my children is dying. He is fifty-eight years old and he has amyotrophic lateral sclerosis or ALS. Most people know this disease as Lou Gehrig's disease because Gehrig, the famous New York Yankee, died from this menace when he was thirty-seven years old. Those of us who know someone who has it call it other things that are not fit to speak in public. And I am here to tell you, there are no lovely rule books that outline how to handle something like this. When you have been divorced for a long time from a man who is now dying and you are watching him die through the eyes of your shared children, the uncharted territory is a maze of anguish that seems immeasurable.

ALS is a progressive neurodegenerative disease that affects nerve cells in the brain and spinal cord. I'm no doctor but what happens is that there is loss of muscle control that eventually affects everything from swallowing and walking to breathing. It is an absolutely horrid way to die. There is no cure, no set cause, and nothing to do really, but watch as a once-vibrant and alive man prepares to die.

I am not the one watching this. I live hundreds of miles away from my children's father and he has made it very clear that this part of his life has nothing to do with me. And he is right about this but he is also terribly wrong.

Can I even say that about a dying man?

This man and I share a son, who is twenty-one years old and a daughter who is nineteen. They are both university students who are excelling at school, in sports, at their jobs and with their own personal relationships. And this, of course, is because they have always had the guiding hand of two parents, albeit two divorced parents, who have loved them and supported them fiercely. It's also a little bit of luck. Sometimes even kids like ours screw up. We hit the flipping jackpot with these two.

When their father was first diagnosed, I felt my lungs collapse and my knees literally dropped to the floor. It had to be a mistake. Maybe it's just a simple tumor, I thought, as I waited with the rest of the world for more test results.

It was no tumor. It was this damn disease and for a while, just a little while, I let the whole thing be all about me. I cried for several days, always when I was not talking to the kids. I did research. I called people and I emailed him. And I could feel a small piece of my heart break off, rattle through my own veins, and move throughout my entire body, as if the sides were scraping across the tops of every single one of my arteries.

The degree of sadness that overtook me, and still rides in my back pocket, was not as astounding to me as it was to some of the other people in my life. "But you've been divorced for such a long time," they would say. Or "I can't believe you are so upset about this. You rarely even speak to him." Or "It's just a shame but it really doesn't have anything to do with you."

How could everyone be so wrong?

Last month my daughter, a long-legged beauty who has her father's eyes, was curled up on my lap while we were watching one of those silly twenty-something gotta-have-a-man movies. We were doing okay until there was a lovely bridal scene and my daughter started to sob uncontrollably. I knew why immediately and she turned to look at me because she couldn't speak.

"Your dad won't be at your wedding, sweetheart," I said through my own tears, "but you know he will be there. He's in your heart. He's always going to be your daddy."

Just a week or so before that, her brother—he also got the hazel eyes but thank God he's got my legs—called very late at night and told me in his hoarse manly whisper that he just needed to talk.

"Mom, oh, Mom, this is so hard and I don't know if I can do this by myself," he sobbed into the phone. "Dad is getting so bad. It's so hard to see this happening. I'm so confused. Help me."

I took the phone into a dark, quiet corner, and we cried together for a very long time and etched out a plan of emails and phone conversations and visits and him making certain he would stay honest with me about when he needed more help. When he wasn't looking I lined up a series of relatives and friends who can guide him, get there quicker than I can, and leave their porch lights on, lend their ears, or whatever he and his sister might need.

And then a few days later my son sent an email begging me to make certain we will always stay close. "If I ever back away, Mom, or if I seem distant, you have to pull me back in. I am so glad you are my mom and my friend. I need you so much."

How can this not be about me, too?

Not so long after I got over, or thought I got over this not being about me at all, I emailed their father again, offered my help and sent a series of notes telling him how I will always honor his memory, his life, his place in the lives and hearts of our children. It was important for me to tell him that, to let him know that all of the anger and hurtful things that have come between us all these years are distant memories—at least for me.

His almost silence, his need to do this his way, was a very loud answer, and although I knew I had to honor whatever he wanted, the feeling of helplessness that came in waves after that was devastating—even as I totally understood it.

I would love to jump in and put up a blind so that our son and daughter do not have to watch their own father die. But I also know I lost the right to have or be or do or say anything. This man has enough on his plate without worrying about an ex-wife for God's sake.

But I am not just an ex-wife. I am also the mother of his children. I am going to be with them on Father's Day next year and the year after that when we will play tennis, and cook a big hunk of meat, and do all of the things he so loved to do in life.

I am the one who is going to remind them how absolutely thrilled he was when they were born and how he put little tennis rackets in their hands and how he was such a whiz at fixing things that he also gave them each a little set of tools.

When they have their own children, and if I am lucky enough to still be around, I will tell them all about their grandpa with nothing but delight and a clear sense of what is important, what is true, what needs to be passed on so that he will always be remembered.

And I will be the rock, the warm arms, the port of warmth and loving understanding as our two babies, our young adults, this man and woman we have both watched grow and struggle and succeed, swim through the oceans of grief that have already covered them way past their knees.

Why are there no rules about this kind of thing?

This week the children are with their father on what most certainly will be the last journey of his life before the big one he has coming up. They are in Alaska, cruising on a ship and making a mess of memories that will have to stretch out and fill in the gaps for many years to come.

I have their itinerary right here by the computer and I look at it several times a day. My daughter is keeping me posted and she is being honest. "It's hard," she admits when she texts me or calls. "He's getting so bad, Mom. It's so sad."

Be strong, is what I say. Feel my heart through all these miles and lean into me. When you want to cry—then cry. Tell him you love him every five seconds, and live your life now and forever with absolutely no regrets. If it is hard for you, my sweet girl, imagine how hard it is for him. And then, of course, I cry like a baby for all three of them.

Watching all of this through the eyes of my children as I stand in the side yard is in a way, an odd gift. It's almost as odd as love itself, that binding force that rises up like a wild unstoppable wind, mixes with compassion, and suddenly erases things that you thought you would never forget or get over.

Lately I have been dreaming about their father almost every night. He's walking slowly in every dream and last night he was carrying a tiny box with his name written on the side. I kept trying to help him, asking him over and over again where he was going and if he needed a ride or something to eat but he would not answer. He kept walking, shuffling his feet, looking straight ahead and he was all alone. When I woke, it was because I heard myself sobbing.

You don't have to be a genius to figure this one out or to know that I have failed miserably in making certain none of this is about me. I hope that the box is full of his precious memories, the jagged and lovely souvenirs of life that one picks up, claims as a treasure, and always remembers no matter how old or young we are when we die.

And if he'd let me, I would slip one very small note in his precious box, so that he might be able to find it one day from whichever cloud he chooses as his new home. My note would say, *"You will always be their father and I will always be their mother."*

About the Author

Kris Radish is the author of nine novels and two works of non-fiction. A former award-winning journalist, magazine writer, nationally syndicated columnist, waitress, worm picker, university lecturer, lifeguard, and professional Girl Scout—to name just a few of her past lives—Radish is also co-owner of a wine lounge, the Wine Madonna, in downtown St. Petersburg, Florida where she hosts books clubs and special literary events with groups from across the globe. Her empowering novels celebrate female friendship, real life, personal empowerment—and naturally, the importance of celebrating life as often as possible. She calls her genre, *Broads Who Have Been There*, and it takes one to know one. Her widely popular novels include *The Elegant Gathering of White Snows, Dancing Naked at the Edge of Dawn, Annie Freeman's Fabulous Traveling Funeral, The Sunday List of Dreams, Searching for Paradise in Parker, PA, The Shortest Distance Between Two Women, Hearts on a String, Tuesday Night Miracles,* and *A Grand Day to Get Lost.* Her tenth novel, *The Year of Necessary Lies* will be published by SparkPress later in 2014.

You can find Kris at:

krisradish.com
facebook.com/kris.radish
twitter.com/krisradish

About SparkPress

SparkPress is an independent boutique publisher delivering high-quality, entertaining, and engaging content that enhances readers' lives, with a special focus on female-driven work. We are proud of our catalog of both fiction and non-fiction titles, featuring authors who represent a wide array of genres, as well as our established, industry-wide reputation for innovative, creative, results-driven success in working with authors. SparkPress, a BookSparks imprint, is a division of SparkPoint Studio, LLC.

To learn more, visit us at sparkpointstudio.com.

CPSIA information can be obtained at www.ICGtesting.com
Printed in the USA
LVOW08s0017280514

387455LV00004B/4/P

9 781940 716435